THE MAJESTIC
Rocky Mountains

By William S. Ellis   *Photographed by* Dick Durrance II

Prepared by the Special Publications Division
National Geographic Society, Washington, D. C.

THE MAJESTIC ROCKY MOUNTAINS
By WILLIAM S. ELLIS,
  National Geographic Staff
Photographed by DICK DURRANCE II,
  National Geographic Photographer

Published by
THE NATIONAL GEOGRAPHIC SOCIETY
MELVIN M. PAYNE, *President*
MELVILLE BELL GROSVENOR, *Editor-in-Chief*
GILBERT M. GROSVENOR, *Editor*

Prepared by
THE SPECIAL PUBLICATIONS DIVISION
ROBERT L. BREEDEN, *Editor*
DONALD J. CRUMP, *Associate Editor*
PHILIP B. SILCOTT, *Senior Editor*
MARY ANN HARRELL, *Managing Editor*
PATRICIA F. FRAKES, SALLIE M. GREENWOOD,
  JENNIFER C. URQUHART, *Research*

Illustrations and Design
DAVID R. BRIDGE, *Picture Editor*
JOSEPHINE B. BOLT, *Art Director*
JOSEPHINE B. BOLT, MARIE A. BRADBY,
  LINDA MCCARTER BRIDGE, WENDY W.
  CORTESI, JACQUELINE GESCHICKTER,
  P. TYRUS HARRINGTON, JANE R.
  MCCAULEY, JUDITH E. RINARD,
  JENNIFER C. URQUHART, *Picture Legends*
JOHN D. GARST, JR., MARGARET A. DEANE,
  TIBOR G. TOTH, ALFRED L. ZEBARTH,
  Map Research, Design, and Production

Production and Printing
ROBERT W. MESSER, *Production Manager*
GEORGE V. WHITE, *Assistant Production*
  Manager
RAJA D. MURSHED, JUNE L. GRAHAM,
  Production Assistants
JOHN R. METCALFE, *Engraving and Printing*
JANE H. BUXTON, STEPHANIE S. COOKE,
  DOROTHY D. FAUST, MARY C. HUMPHREYS,
  SUZANNE J. JACOBSON, SANDRA LEE
  MATTHEWS, VIRGINIA A. MCCOY, SELINA
  R. M. PATTON, MARILYN L. WILBUR,
  Staff Assistants
BARBARA L. KLEIN, *Index*

*Early-morning skiers descend a 3,000-foot
slope in the "Bugaboos," part of the Purcell
Mountains in British Columbia. Overleaf:
Snow-swept Absaroka Range rises east of
Paradise Valley, Montana. Page 1: A Rocky
Mountain bighorn sheep roams the wilderness.
Bookbinding: A mountain chickadee searches
for insects in the bark of a piñon twig.*

FOREWORD

Nothing in the world seems as enduring as a great rampart of mountain rising in a morning light—the wall of the Front Range beyond Denver, the Wasatch over Salt Lake City, the Continental Ranges at Jasper. And yet, when viewed closely, there are few things more fragile than mountains and the life they sustain.

In recent years, with the vastly increased popularity of downhill and cross-country skiing, backpacking, and climbing, millions of Americans have rediscovered our mountains. They cherish the beauty of solitude, the joy of the pure air and sweeping vistas from a lonely summit. But this awareness extracts its price.

On a recent visit to Jasper National Park, in Canada, I fumed for two hours in a traffic jam; yet next morning I set out on horseback for the wilderness near Mount Robson. For ten days our party encountered waterfalls, high meadows, mountain streams—and exactly three other people.

Last year, while in the Teton Range with Dr. Frank Craighead, I rappelled down a cliff to behold a nest of golden eaglets, and a scant hour or two later was surrounded by the billboards and busy streets of Jackson.

Everywhere, it seems, our search for the restorative strength of the great mountains is accompanied by land speculation, hard-pressed water systems, inadequate sewer systems, and environmental degradation at the gates of the wilderness. And that is an important theme of this book: what we risk if we strip the mountains bare of timber, or gut the Rockies for minerals.

Photographer Dick Durrance, reared in Colorado, shows us the splendor of unspoiled high country and the fast-changing human scene of the 1970's. His pictures convey what is at stake in the Rockies for an energy-hungry nation and for those who call the region home. As author Bill Ellis says, this book is "a view from today."

Bill has had an affinity for the Rockies since his first newspaper job in Lewistown, Montana, two decades ago. He understands overcrowding and rampant growth, clear cuts and strip mines. He looks upon the mountains with deep respect, as did the Indians who called them "hoary-headed fathers." In a way they are like wise old men, offering wisdom through beauty and solitude, marked by the patience of the ages; but, in the end, they are vulnerable. Their destiny is up to us.

Mountain man Jim Bridger once remarked: "A man kin see so much farther in that country." I hope that readers of this book will also be able to see farther from these pages, to a time when man and mountain live in balance.

GILBERT M. GROSVENOR

CONTENTS

M̄an of mountain ways, José Fernandez

has lived all his 78 years in the Rockies—as miner, cattle rancher, sheepman.

CHAPTER ONE

A Past of Turmoil: The Shaping of the Ranges

SOON, THE ROCKIES. Even now they are in view, although distance dulls the sharpness of the peaks until they stand rounded and gentle against the horizon. Before another nightfall I shall have left the Great Plains and the last emerald field of ripening corn behind me. It has been a drive of anticipation—of waiting for the vista (even if obscured by the scarlet and purple carnage of summer bugs on the windshield) of a continent cresting in snow-dusted waves of granite.

My approach is to the Front Range of the Rockies, where Denver and Colorado Springs and Boulder press against the foothills. Prominent among the mountains in this range is Pikes Peak, not the highest at 14,110 feet, but the one prospectors looked to as a landmark when journeying westward in the 1850's in quest of gold.

The mountain takes its name from Zebulon Montgomery Pike, an Army officer whose short life was a catalogue of bad luck. His exploits in the West failed to win the acclaim he felt was due; rather, he returned to find himself a suspect in the hubbub of rumors that Aaron Burr was conspiring to set up a western republic of his own. Eager to market his journals, he chose a publisher who soon went bankrupt. Finally, at the age of 34, in the War of 1812, Zebulon Pike died of wounds received in the explosion of a powder magazine.

But at two o'clock in the afternoon of November 15, 1806, he did one thing right: He looked through his spyglass and identified what appeared to be "a small blue cloud" as a mountain—a mountain he and his men would pursue for days, even through snow that reached to the waist. At one point Pike estimated they had only 15 miles to go. It was more like 50.

"The summit of the Grand Peak, which was entirely bare of vegetation and covered with snow, now appeared at the distance of

Time-congealed lava, not one foot high, curls like a wave at Craters of the Moon National Monument in Idaho. Here successive lava floods built up a vast plateau—minor, recent incidents in the long saga of the Rockies.

15 or 16 miles from us," he wrote, ". . . and would have taken a whole day's march to have arrived at its base, when I believe no human being could have ascended to its pinical."

Well, a human being *could* reach the summit, as Dr. Edwin James and friends were the first to do, in 1820. Indeed, there is now a road or a cog railway to the top for those who choose not to walk.

The mountain is a fitting frontispiece for the Rockies. Rising with style and authority, it sets a proper mood—a sense of wonder and submissiveness—for this vast swath of high country.

I have been with these mountains in all seasons, in weather both violent and benign, at places where the land reaches far above tree line and snow survives July. Sometimes I denounced, with conviction, the myth that the nobility of mountains rubs off on those who climb them. There is nothing noble in frostbite. I have even sworn allegiance to the memory of Charles Lamb for a thought he once penned to William Wordsworth: "Separate from the pleasure of your company, I don't much care if I never see a mountain in my life."

But such reactions were short-lived. I endured the cold to watch a golden eagle soar across a canyon on wings spanning seven feet, and it was worth it. I reeled with dizziness in the thin air at 14,000 feet to fill my soul with wilderness solitude. And it was worth it.

FOR THOSE CAUGHT UP in the first of the 19th-century treasure-hunting sweeps across the continent, the mountains, like cholera and Indians, were hazards to be done with as quickly and as painlessly as possible. Even later, when the Rockies were found to hold their own mineral riches, the hordes came to take and get out, setting a pattern of exploitation that would plague the Mountain West for years to come.

Of course there were hardships. Men torn from their families by the lure of gold carried a heavy burden of loneliness. But if a prospector longed to hear the church bell of a New England village on Sunday morning, his determination to grab off a share of the wealth was even greater. Make it big and then go home—that was the dream shared by most. Certainly, Harry Faulkner dreamed that, for this is what he wrote in a letter to his children:

"I am soon going over a great big river, and then away off to a place where there aint any people living. There are no houses there, only tents that are made out of cloth . . . and keep out the rain. That is the place that they call Pike's Peak. There is lots of gold there, and that is what money is made out of. I will get some when I go there, and bring some home to you and ma. I was sorry to hear that little Metta was sick. . . . I will bring her lots of the prettyest kind of rings, and will bring Harry something nice, too, if you are both good, and will mind ma all the time. I look at your pictures every day. . . . Tell ma to write pa a letter. Good bye, dear children."

That was in 1859. Harry Faulkner spent months seeking his fortune. Evidently, he failed. His diary, now in the Denver Public Library, does not reveal what he decided to do. So, I wonder: Did he stay in the Rockies, and did his family join him there? Did he take Metta to the top of a mountain and show her the blue-white of alpine forget-me-not in bloom? She would then have forgiven him, I think, for not finding gold and buying her lots of the prettiest kind of rings.

At one point, Faulkner visited Auraria—a forerunner of Denver—and saw people leaving "in crowds." Staking a claim right there would have been a sound move, for the city would take fire with activity and growth. It would become the hub of a mountain empire.

Denver sits just east of the southern Rockies—that is, the southern part of the Rockies in the United States. The Rockies themselves are the eastern part of the North American Cordillera, the great mountain system that extends from the Brooks Range in Alaska through Canada and the United States southward into Mexico.

Sharpening the focus, the main body of the system carries from Santa Fe to the Canadian border, and then for 420 miles north along the boundary between British Columbia and Alberta. With this as my route, my travels touched on six states—New Mexico, Colorado, Utah, Wyoming, Idaho, and Montana—in addition to the two Canadian provinces.

Here rises the true crest of this broad land—the Continental Divide. (Is that not a name for inscription on parchment?) It is not a sharply defined spine of ridge. It follows an erratic course, running along the summit of a mountain several miles above sea level, or, in another area, crossing an interstate highway with only a slight rise to hint at its presence. In the Wyoming Basin, largest in the Rockies with 40,000 square miles, it may be nearly undetectable to the eye.

Yet everywhere it divides the waters of the continent. Even as a gentle rise of ground, it is a barrier that no river breaches. Instead, water flows away from it, with drainage on the west going to the Pacific and on the east to the Arctic or the Atlantic.

There is majesty as well as brilliance in the concept. Consider this: A flush of spring warmth sets off snow melt on an eastern slope. The water is soon caught up within a minor stream and later, having advanced to a creek, it tumbles through the shade of willows and cottonwoods. This eventually carries into a river—say, the Missouri—and from there to the Gulf of Mexico. Finally, the meltwater enters

Slain by Indians, a "fifty-niner" lies beside his wagon—an artist's comment on a boom that broke the hopes of many. Thousands rushed to the Pikes Peak area in 1859 when prospectors found gold nearby—only to leave saying, "Busted, by God."

the Atlantic Ocean. Along the way on the 4,000-mile journey, it probably went berserk in rapids, cascaded over a fall, bumped into a beaver, and washed away a bit of a flatlands farm.

The Continental Divide, linchpin for this feat of waterway engineering, was born with the mountains, born of violence in the earth. Indeed, to account for the Rockies by up-to-date explanations, nothing less than a continent is required—and a continent in motion at that.

The notion of continents adrift is far from new; but a generally accepted theory has evolved within the past twenty years and acquired fame under the label "plate tectonics" in the past five or six. As the noted geophysicist Dr. Leon Knopoff has written, "Teaching of geology is being totally revised."

IN THIS NEW VIEW, the crust of the earth—once believed to be a rigid shell—is an assortment of giant plates of rock, plates 30 to 100 miles thick and as large as North America. These plates slide slowly over hot and yielding rock beneath them. They move while magma, or molten rock, wells up at rifts within the oceans and the sea floor spreads outward on either side; and at times they jostle and collide.

Such encounters produce dramatic results in their immediate vicinity. California's coastal mountains and the notorious San Andreas Fault system seem obvious products of one: The North American plate, moving westward from the Mid-Atlantic Ridge, sideswipes the floor of the Pacific as that plate moves northwestward.

What role did this play in the birth of the Rockies? The answer is not obvious. A committee of specialists has warned that the Rockies, "although impressive in dimensions, are not located along plate boundaries" and do not closely resemble such ranges as the Andes. They form a distinct tectonic unit, and have for millennia.

Some of the rock in these ranges dates from two billion years ago: the so-called "basement rock" of the continent, that composes the Canadian Shield. In Colorado, for example, at Black Canyon of the Gunnison National Monument, the great cliff called the Painted Wall exposes rock older than 1.7 billion years. Such rock has endured many cycles of change.

Off and on for millions—hundreds of millions—of years, the West was covered by a succession of shallow inland seas. Thick layers of sediment would form as debris washed down from adjacent highlands. In places, sediment would accumulate to a thickness of 18 miles, with the original sea bed sinking beneath it. Then the area would find a new equilibrium, with the surface buckling into mountains. Yet even as the mountains were rising, the forces of erosion were at work, with wind and water cutting away at the rock until not even hills remained. And then the sea would return.

Heartland of the Mountain West, the Rockies form the eastern portion of the North American Cordillera—a vast and crumpled region. Youngest of the nation's mountains, they hold some of its most prized resources.

"Mountains are only temporary features. They're constantly destroying themselves," says Dr. Mel Griffiths with the calm that geologists seem to acquire from the scope of their studies. (Brought up in the Rockies, a mountain climber and a licensed pilot, he is now professor of geography at the University of Denver.) But the rate of self-destruction varies, he explains. Erosion varies with elevation, climate, and many other factors; and uplift may compensate for it.

"You remember Alice in Looking Glass land—she had to run as fast as she could just to stay in the same place. Well, a mountain may have to rise as fast as it can just to keep the same height." Thus it could take 5,000 years for a mountain to suffer a net loss of one inch through erosion.

"Alice should have studied geology," he adds. "She insisted that 'a hill *can't* be a valley' because that would be nonsense." But the cycle of mountain-and-valley has recurred countless times.

There is evidence of a great uplift between 300 and 250 million years ago, resulting in the formation of the so-called Ancestral Rockies, mountains that extended east to Oklahoma. It took some 50 million years for erosion to cut them down.

THEN, millions of years later, began an immense geological disturbance known as the Laramide Revolution or Laramide orogeny (literally, birth of mountains). "It disturbed everything west of the central plains, from the Brooks Range down into Mexico," says Dr. Griffiths, "and it must be a result of plate movement because it affected such a wide area within the same span of time. Generally, it involved the effect we compare to rumpling a rug, with intense folding near the Pacific Coast—the most rumpling of the rug, so to speak, where it's pushed against the wall of the Pacific plate. But things are more complicated in the Rockies.

"Almost every range of the Rockies has its own special characteristics," he says happily, "and therefore it needs a unique, discrete set of explanations."

These unique explanations are a specialty of Dr. Ogden Tweto's. He has worked for the U. S. Geological Survey for 36 years, and ranks as an authority on the southern Rockies. I met him in his office on the outskirts of Denver, in one of those faceless government buildings where the corridors always seem to end in the wrong places.

"Creation of the Rocky Mountains here in Colorado began about 70 million years ago—later than to the west and north of us," he said. "They continued to build for some millions of years, but were pretty well worn down by about 45 million years ago." He picked up a steel ruler and jabbed a relief map of the southern Rockies as he talked.

"There was a gigantic volcanic episode about 40 million years ago, and that created the San Juan Mountains. As the volcanic activity started to die out, after 15 million years or so, there was great faulting. One faulted edge left standing is now the Sangre de Cristo Mountains." He lighted a cigarette and squeezed past filing cabinets and a draftsman's board to get to his desk and continue his chronicle.

Following an afternoon with Tweto, I came away with a kaleidoscope of mental pictures from that long spectacular past—of the marine transgressions, or invasions by the seas, with vast swampy areas near their shores. Ferns appeared, for the climate was mild. Animals with a reach of neck as high as a telephone pole roamed about with a plant-eater's oafish indifference to everything except food — or the need to escape some carnivorous and hungry foe. Of course, not all dinosaurs were large. Some matured no bigger than a pheasant. But others left immense three-toed footprints — a birdlike print three feet long would prove that a tyrannosaur was here, a big one. Some, the sauropods, left footprints resembling an elephant's. These beasts had odd proportions. *Diplodocus,* for example, on its four massive legs, had a wheelbase about the size of a big elephant's; but thirty feet of long slim neck wavered in front of the body, and forty feet of long skinny tail dragged behind it.

Millions of years later, the swamps where the dinosaurs fed would draw the attention of a nation running short on sources of energy. The accumulation of peat and fossil plant material had aged into extensive deposits of coal. And from the ancient lakes would emerge shale laced with the greatest reserve of oil in the world.

With the disappearance of the tepid seas and the inexorable rise of new mountains, the million-century reign of the giant reptiles reached its obscure conclusion. Masses of already-ancient granite edged higher. Warped surfaces of rock fractured and folded yet again. Fissures in the earth spewed up lava that coalesced into plateaus.

The Laramide orogeny came to its close with the waning of the epoch called Eocene, "the dawn of the recent." Camels and three-toed horses roamed the land, and here and there a poplar tree grew.

The mountains did not emerge as we know them today. Erosion would alter their appearance — chipping, boring, biting, hacking like some mad sculptor working for a portrait in dust. The breaking-down process continues even now, of course, and can be observed at work whenever a rock, no matter how small, tumbles down a slope.

Gravity maintains its steady force. Winds vary their attack — wind driving sand against soft stone can reduce it quickly. Water turbid with sediment carves out canyons. Frost wedging loosens rock from its place. But the greatest agent shaping the high mountains to their present contour has been ice.

The Ice Age began about two million years ago in the Rockies, with the last retreat of the glaciers occurring as recently as eight or ten thousand years ago. There were at least three episodes of glaci-ation, with immense ice sheets advancing southward from the Arctic, and separate masses of ice forming on individual ranges. The ice moved slowly — a few feet a year was commonplace — but with power enough to undermine a mountain wall.

A mountain glacier started to slide when the ice reached a cer-tain thickness: say, well over a hundred feet. Picking up debris as it moved, the glacier would grind the surface beneath it to a polish. It would plane away the jaggedness of cliffs and round off the angles of a valley. Often, at its mountain headwall, the mass of ice would quarry an amphitheater out of bedrock, and this would be called a cirque. The waters now filling these scalloped hollows are among the loveliest of hidden mountain lakes.

And so they came, three times (maybe more) down the mountains, to give the Rockies much of their present lordly character. Only the sun could stop their advance, and the sites of death-by-melt are marked today by moraines, the piles of rock and earth carried along on the slow journey through the cold.

The mountains stand, then, much as they did at the end of the Ice Age—and with much the same fauna, including the bighorn and the mountain goat. During some interval between the spread of ice sheets, bison had made their way from Asia. And human hunters had established themselves and their families on the continent, roaming south of the ice sheet and, presumably, exploring the country it left clear. To journey from the south may be to follow them.

Starting, then, in the south, the Sangre de Cristo Mountains run for 220 miles. High in their youthful reaches are exceedingly ancient rocks, jumbled up to overlie later ones by the flamboyance of creation in the Mountain West. Rising boldly out of the New Mexico lowlands, these peaks at sunset are chapels of color, mostly red; thus the name, which translates from the Spanish as "the Blood of Christ." Among the subranges is the Taos with the highest mountain in New Mexico, Wheeler Peak: 13,161 feet. To climb Wheeler Peak, as I had the good fortune to do in spring, is to pass through all the life zones of growth, from desert sagebrush to alpine lichen.

DESERT SANDS, flicked by the wind and driven into great dunes, pile against the slopes of the Sangre de Cristos; but soon forests take over the terrain. Within 75 miles to the west the mountains called San Juan rise out of a striking spread of pine. Crossing into Colorado, the broad San Juan range pushes through a land so primitive as to be intimidating.

These are mountains born of volcanic accumulations in an area of uplift, with canyon walls polished by glaciers that scooped out the U-shaped valleys. Durango and Silverton and Pagosa Springs sit here as boots-and-saddle western towns in the full glow of mountain splendor. Here too, Wolf Creek Pass collects as much as 800 inches of snow in winter as it notches the Continental Divide at 10,857 feet.

The San Juan National Forest includes some of the namesake mountains and part of a formally designated wilderness, the Weminuche. Federal law reserves such areas for "the earth and its community of life." In this 405,031-acre expanse grow ponderosa pine and Douglas fir, quaking aspen and spruce. Marsh marigolds and orchids flourish at heights up to 10,000 feet; while higher, in subalpine conditions, columbine brightens the rock-strewn meadows.

It is north of the San Juans, where a great anticlinal fold gives elevation to the Sawatch Range, that the Rockies are highest. Mount Elbert is first in height at 14,433 feet, followed by Mount Massive at 14,421 and Mount Harvard at 14,420. Such exact figures should be taken with caution, warns Dr. Tweto; some peaks have been measured "plus or minus five feet." With that caveat, then, more than fifty peaks of the Rockies exceed 14,000 feet. All are in Colorado.

West of the Sawatch Range lie remnants of sedimentary layers stripped away long since from above its crest. And to the east, near

Colorado Springs, that sandstone has survived the Laramide events to form the Garden of the Gods. Grotesque masses of red stone impose themselves upon the landscape. Helen Hunt Jackson, a 19th-century novelist, called them "colossal monstrosities . . . all motionless and silent, with a strange look of having been just stopped and held back in the very climax of some supernatural catastrophe."

The Garden of the Gods can also be seen, I suppose, as some earth force in a horror mask lunging out to startle and astonish. How would those earliest human visitors have understood this place?

There the procession of mountains continues, north into Wyoming with the Medicine Bow range. The Uinta and Wasatch ranges fill northeastern and central Utah with a purplish-gray grandeur. Erosion played one of its subtler pranks here, as Dr. Griffiths explains it: "We have about 40,000 feet of measured uplift — and just about its equivalent in sediments removed by the Green River and the headstreams of the Colorado. You find it down in the Gulf of California."

Northward again, the older hump-shouldered ranges of the Rockies march up the length of Idaho. These uniform ranges were

Bringing precision to exploring, a Hayden Survey team maps the Rockies. With tripod and transit, topographer George B. Chittenden computes elevations and distances. His partner W. H. Holmes sketches the terrain. Data collected from 1867 to 1878, with the results of three other "great surveys," gave the nation its first scientific appraisal of the resources of the Mountain West.

worn from a massive batholith of granite, with deep narrow valleys.

Then, Montana. Montana's linear ranges shaped by faulting and overthrust. The Absarokas, volcanic work again. Here the complex geology of the Laramide Revolution fashioned a portion of America to inspire songs of gladness. Admittedly, I am prejudiced. Off and on, for more than twenty years, I have been drawn back to Montana, and I suspect that I will never lose my affection for that state.

To drive north out of Yellowstone National Park, through the Paradise Valley to Bozeman and west to Three Forks, past mile after mile of unbroken range fence, past the dark chambers of pine forests, past a dozen sad and silent towns (their names are lost) that knot the highway to Missoula—that, to me, is the most pleasurable way to fall into the embrace of the Rockies.

As they move north, the Rockies lose height. Near Butte, the Continental Divide averages 6,000 feet above sea level. However, the mountains are gathered together in a grand convention of scenery. In place after place along these ranges—the Bitterroot, Mission, Flat-head, Gallatin, and others—there are sights to evoke a bygone way of life. Twenty miles west of Bozeman, for example, there are hills where buffalo were stampeded, forced to leap to their death on the slopes below. I stood there on a November day sullen and gray with the promise of snow, and envisioned the scene. . . .

Driven by hunters of the Blackfeet tribe, the great beasts rumble toward the jump. Near the edge, the animals in the lead suddenly sense the danger and attempt to turn. It is too late; they are caught up in the onrush of the herd and carried to their death. Quickly, the Blackfeet women are there with stone knives, removing the skins with flicking, flashing dexterity.

Of course, there are buffalo jumps in many parts of the Mountain West, but only in Montana, it seems to me, can the faint echoes of the terrible bone-crushing falls still be heard.

The Rockies carry the Continental Divide into Canada by way of Waterton-Glacier International Peace Park, and thereafter for 300 miles the mountains traverse a succession of Canadian parks. Best known, indeed world famous, are the travel-poster classics of Banff and Jasper National Parks, in the Continental Ranges; to the north lies uncluttered country where development is not even thought of. Mount Robson, at 12,972 feet, marks the highest summit in the Canadian Rockies; by convention, the Liard River marks their northern limit, though the immense mountain system does not end.

To the west it enjoys a clear boundary: a great valley nearly 900 miles long from Kalispell, Montana, to the Liard Plain, a valley so sharply defined that it earns the name of Rocky Mountain Trench. West of it are noble mountains, but the contorted evidence of the Laramide turmoil catches the geologist's eye on the Rockies' side.

Other eyes see things differently. Skiers cheerfully cross the trench by helicopter from Banff to reach the glaciers of the Selkirk range. And I followed a Canadian's tip and crossed it to find a place I was hoping for: a little town where bureaucracy does not dwarf the human scale of living and nothing blurs the view. It was a resident from Revelstoke, which surely has one of the most beautiful settings anywhere on earth, who gave me the suggestion, "If you're looking for a beautiful town, you should go over to Kaslo."

Kaslo's citizens are not given to bragging, and some are quick to say, "We're in the Selkirks, you know." But to my mind they're proof (if any is needed) that the values of the Mountain West are to be acclaimed wherever you find them.

OF ALL THE RANGES in the Rockies, in my opinion, one stands alone in self-assertion. It is the Teton Range. The jagged, storm-wracked Tetons thrust into the western sky above the Wyoming valley called Jackson Hole. These mountains and this valley have been called the most spectacular feast of scenery in the country.

The Tetons, mountains without foothills, were formed by fault-block action. One block was uplifted and tilted along a fault zone, while its counterpart across the zone was dropped. The highest edge became the steep, rugged face that the Tetons turn to the east. The dropped block became Jackson Hole.

The Tetons may still be rising, at an estimated rate of one foot every 500 years, and the valley still be sinking—in the past 15,000 years it is believed to have dropped 150 feet. But it isn't easy to assess the status of mountains floating on an unstable continent.

"We tend to assume that a mountain goes on doing what it has been doing," says Dr. Griffiths, "but we can't be positive. We don't have a plane of reference. We don't have a skyhook."

Clearly, however, activity continues within a seismic belt that extends well south and north of the Tetons. Indeed, at nearby Yellowstone National Park seismographs record a surprising number of disturbances in the mountainous earth—more than 400 in just the first 20 days of 1975. Most are as gentle as a hiccup, while others rattle dishes and spook wildlife. At least one caused a mountain to fall.

On August 17, 1959, a Monday, an earthquake centered a few miles west of the park wrenched a large area of the northern Rockies with such force that the face of a mountain in the Madison Range was dislodged, sending 80 million tons of rock crashing down into a river. Water backed up behind the barrier and formed a lake. Elsewhere, peaks trembled, sending down more rock. Highway pavement ripped like an old shirt or cracked into chunks. Within the park, new geysers erupted, and a few of the old ones settled down to new schedules after a frenzied "wild phase."

Such events make this an ideal research zone for the earth sciences, but not an easy one. In the late 1960's a U. S. Geological Survey team drilled 1,088 feet down at Norris Geyser Basin and found a temperature of 465° F., past the melting point of tin. The crew began to consider the possibility of their equipment's being hurled up out of the ground by high-pressure steam. They stopped, and one has explained that "Frankly, we're chicken."

Today the scientists working at Yellowstone spend a fair bit of time arguing over variations of plate theory, such as the idea that an "undigested" fragment or two of the Pacific plate may underlie the western states. As yet, cautions one, "nothing's been proved."

Meanwhile, nature's routine assaults on the Rockies are sometimes devastating and consistently frequent. On a winter night in Kalispell, the plastic drinking glasses in my motel room fell off the dresser when an earthquake that measured five on the Mercalli scale shook the town. Snow was piling up outside to a depth of almost a foot while an announcer on the radio reported a blizzard about to strike.

Partly because of such conditions, it took almost four centuries to get the Mountain West in governable order as civilization understood it. Starting in 1540 with the arrival in the southern Rockies of Captain-General Francisco Vásquez de Coronado, the Spanish explorer, and ending near the turn of the current century with the coming of the railroads and the fencing of the ranges, attempts at settlement were cursed as often as not with the certainty of failure.

It was the demands of the marketplace that drove many to the mountains. They came for the beaver pelts needed to make hats. They came for gold. They came because the railroads offered work.

Throughout much of the national history, development of the Mountain West drew its impetus from greed. Territories gained statehood, but even then they had little control over their destinies. The vast region was, and to a large extent still is, a citizen-held trust: federal land, federal direction, and, alas, federal indifference. In no other region, I believe, does distrust of the federal government run as deep as in the Mountain West.

Today the nation has new demands and the states of the Rockies stand to be bludgeoned with affection. The need now is for energy. And the resources are there, in the great beds of coal and oil shale.

The Mountain West, for the most part, is no longer willing to submit to exploitation. Many who live there regard the quality of life as extraordinarily good. A child in, say, Driggs, Idaho, leaves the house for school in the morning and has the thrill of seeing a moose feeding on the front lawn. A Philadelphian relocated in Polson, Montana, finds that breathing need not be painful. Families picnic in the mountain meadows that are their backyards.

This, then, is where the battle lines are being drawn today: quality of life versus industrialization and prosperity. There have already been some skirmishes.

Alert for scalding steam from Lion Geyser, geochemist Mike Thompson collects a water sample in Yellowstone National Park. He calls the park "the best natural lab in the world" for geothermal studies, and joins in a United Nations project to utilize such energy in poorer nations.

Giant sandstone pillars and jagged spires fill the Garden of the Gods in central Colorado, once the bed of long-vanished seas. The Garden took shape some 70 million years ago

in a phase of uplift that raised and tilted and gnarled its rocks as new mountains rose. Wind and water have sculpted it in the slow, relentless cycle of earth's change.

*A*thabasca Glacier, darkened by rock debris, sprawls two-thirds of a mile wide in
Canada's Jasper National Park. Moving slowly downhill, glaciers carve the distinctive U-
shaped valleys common in the Rockies. Athabasca's meltwaters eventually reach the Arctic
Ocean; glacier melt gives year-round chill to the famous emerald waters of Lake Louise.

Through this now-serene land, the Wyoming Basin, runs the Continental Divide. Here sediment eroded from the newly formed Rockies began filling an ancient lake bed

...bout 60 or 65 million years ago. On the distant plain the Boars Tusk rises 395 feet, ...va plug from a volcanic cone worn away by erosion's agents—wind and water.

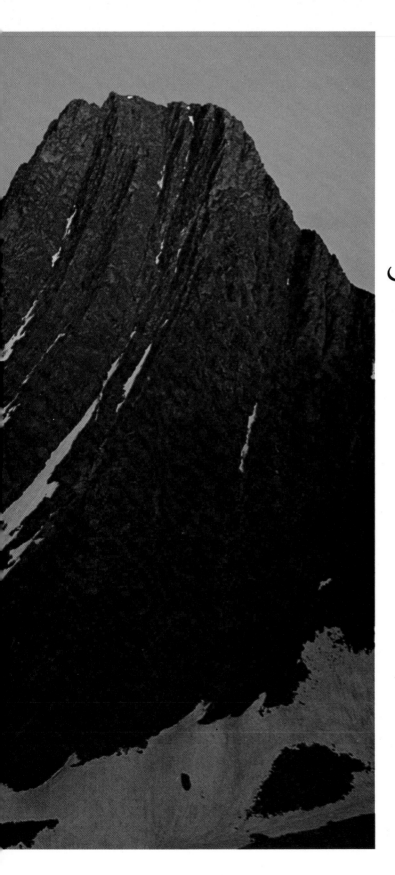

At twilight, a pale moon rises over the Grenadier Range in southwestern Colorado—with Vestal Peak dominant at 13,644 feet. Snow lingers between hard strata of quartzite that resisted glacial erosion during the past million years. Building mountains—and wearing them away—involves complex processes measured in epochs. The Grenadiers, with other ranges of the San Juans, probably began rising 70 million years ago. Geologists think the earth's crust contains giant plates of rock set in motion by heat from the interior. When plates collide and compress the crust, it wrinkles old rock into new mountains. The rocks now visible on Vestal Peak date from 1,500 million years ago.

*S*unlight clearing the Sangre de Cristo range brings morning to Colorado's Great Sand

Dunes National Monument. Wind has rippled the sand eroded from the San Juan Mountains.

CHAPTER TWO

A West Wild with Riches: Boom Times Past and Present

M Y CAR HAD BROKEN DOWN on Interstate 80, and the first vehicle to come along stopped to give me a ride. It was a fine pickup, a green two-ton Ford with a black Labrador retriever in the back. A sticker on the rear bumper proclaimed that COWBOYS DO IT BETTER.

We were 50 miles out of Rock Springs, in the reach of scrubby desert across south-central Wyoming. This is land of great emptiness, sorrowful land where wind-scoured buttes rise like bad growths. Forty miles back, the highway crosses the Continental Divide, and if one has the urge, he or she can stand there, on that gentle swell in the macadam, and become filled with the truth of a geological miracle.

"Broke down once myself, about in the same place," the driver told me. "Damn near died of heat stroke waiting for a ride." He was a man of, I'd guess, 60. His fat, tobacco-stained fingers were like smoked sausages as they gripped the wheel to guide the pickup back onto the highway. The dog stood on the bed of the truck and let the rush of wind break across her broad face. Her name, I learned, was Lillian. She was three years old, and a crackerjack swimmer.

It was a pleasurable drive because, for one thing, I like pickup trucks. They are the Conestoga wagons of our time, and to drive one in the Mountain West is to gain a sense of frontiersmanship. Also, it seems to me that the pickup is the best arrangement of steel yet devised for the service of those who take livelihoods from the land.

The driver, who said he's called Buck, sat high in the cab of the truck. He slid his broadbrimmed hat back, scratched his head, and said the West he had known, man and boy, was changing. "But we're still pretty much at the mercy of the politicians in Washington," he said. "The Secretary of the Interior is the president of the country as far as we're concerned. All those agencies under his control—

Clad in heat-reflecting gear, a worker checks the temperature of molten copper—about 1,500° F.—at a smelter of the Anaconda Company, still a leading employer and long a dominant force within Montana.

Bureau of Land Management, Bureau of Mines, National Parks—call most of the shots out here, but we're not going to let them push us around anymore without a fight."

He broke off to yell at Lillian because she was barking at the motorcycle passing us. I asked how he felt about the way the government has been managing the vast public lands in the West.

"I'll put it to you this way," he replied. "I think the last thing the government did right was to win World War II. Hush up, Lillian!"

Buck's anger with the federal government was most pronounced when he talked about its restrictions on the killing of coyotes. As a sheep rancher, he said, he had lost plenty of money in recent years because of damage by coyotes.

"The government protects the coyotes, and now they're everywhere. Sometimes there's as many as 12 pups in a litter of coyotes." He slapped the palm of his hand against the wheel. "I'd like to get some of them wildlife nuts out at my place and make them watch a coyote grab a lamb by the throat and rip it apart. Now, you tell me, how come there ain't no lamb-lovers in the government?"

Traffic was getting heavy, and Buck said we'd probably hit Rock Springs just in time for the rush.

" 'What rush?' When's the last time you're there?"

"Eight, nine years ago."

"You won't believe it when you see it."

I remembered Rock Springs as a town in the throes of despair and decay. There was a grayness about the place, a forlorn quality that carried through the streets. It was a town with a mission in life: to supply the Union Pacific Railroad with coal from the local mines. But with the switch to diesel engines in the 1950's there was no longer much reason for freights to stop. Rock Springs was passed by.

But it still had the coal. Clean-burning and low in sulphur, it lay in thick beds across more than 95 percent of the county—a county larger than Rhode Island *and* Massachusetts. To a nation running short of sources of energy, Rock Springs and Sweetwater County had something to offer. So change came to the town.

UP AHEAD, cars and trucks by the hundred are entering the highway from a side road. It's a little after 4:30 p.m.—end of a work shift at the new power plant. Thirty-five miles away, Rock Springs waits for the workers. Bartenders wait to start pouring the drinks. Doctors wait to start patching the wounds scored in brawls. Police wait to start rolling on the calls.

Rock Springs is in the grip of a sudden boom. Economically, it's a benediction; socially, a curse. Rock Springs prospers at the expense of damage to the quality of life. Elsewhere in the Rocky Mountain region, other communities must make choices in such matters. Twenty years ago—no, ten—their right of self-determination was not to be assumed. Even now it may not be wise to take it for granted.

Buck drops me at a motel, a rambling complex of rooms opened in the past six months. Across the highway sits another new motel. There are others, too, and the whole area at twilight is afire with the reds and yellows of neon: VACANCY, NO VACANCY, LIVE ENTERTAIN-

I must wait an hour or so for my room because there is a shortage of cleaning women.

That evening, in the dining room of the motel, I talk with the family at the table next to mine and learn that the man earns seven dollars an hour at the power plant. He and his wife and two children drove to Rock Springs from Florida in a 1963 station wagon. Unable to find rental housing, and having spent their meager savings on gas and repairs, they slept in the wagon for two weeks. Now they have one of the thousands of house trailers crowded onto lots in and around the city. Of all the tawdry spinoffs of the busyness in Rock Springs, none is more visible than the mobile home.

"By the summer of 1973, 3,500 workers had come tumbling into town when we were told to expect 1,200," says Charles Richardson, editor-publisher of the *Rock Springs Daily Rocket-Miner*. "We weren't ready for that. A lot of things got out of hand, including crime. We used to print individual stories on crimes, but now we just run them in a list."

Even as he speaks, a reporter is preparing the list for tomorrow's paper. It includes a report of the theft of all the furniture, clothing, dishes, linens — everything — from a trailer house. The owner's dog, a not-so-watchful German shepherd, was also taken.

Rock Springs boomed in the past few years because the Idaho Power Co. and the Pacific Power & Light Co. had decided to manufacture electricity in Sweetwater County, using strip-mined coal to fuel the generators. The jointly owned plant would be located near the midpoint of the strip, still called the "mouth" of the mine. The cost as originally estimated: 800 million dollars. As currently estimated, 900 million dollars including the transmission lines.

At the same time, accelerated activity in the trona mines continued. Trona is an evaporite mineral used in the manufacture of various products, including bicarbonate of soda. Sweetwater County has the largest reserve of trona in the country. In fact, the Green River area of Wyoming has by far the largest deposits in the world, an estimated 80 billion tons — certainly enough to cure the heartburns of the populace for centuries to come.

Work began in 1970 on the first of four generating units at the power plant, and it started transmitting in November 1974. The production capacity of just one of the units (500,000 kilowatts) is sufficient to meet present electrical needs for all of Wyoming. But the power isn't meant for Wyoming; it will be sent to the Northwest, for use in Oregon, Washington, and Idaho.

"This is an ideal site for a power plant," Kenneth W. Worrall, construction auditor for the project, tells me. "The coal seams here are 28 to 30 feet thick and they stretch for 16 miles. It makes for a good strip-mining operation." The power companies, he stresses, will repair damages to the land. Mined areas will be backfilled, and the surface, with topsoil replaced, will be contoured and replanted. Nothing less would be acceptable, not in the Mountain West of today where concern for the environment is a force to be reckoned with.

Trona mining, an underground procedure, does little damage.

Dragging lumber to shore up mine tunnels, freight mules file through Telluride, Colorado—nicknamed "city of gold" in the 1880's. Today a ski resort lies among mountains that once yielded millions.

Nothing enters the streams and only natural elements of dust go into the air. Strip mining is notoriously more controversial. And just recently the power industry's new high-voltage transmission lines have stirred new questions. Such lines are surrounded by electrical fields; environmentalists and health specialists fear possible adverse effects on any people in their vicinity.

Meanwhile, the social impact of industry on Sweetwater County raises concerns of its own. One federal official foresees ten years of "chaotic conditions" but a stable community thereafter. Ken Worrall thinks the coal seams near the new plant will last thirty-five years; after that another plant could replace it on seams nearby.

It is Friday night and a $700,000 payroll has been turned loose among more than 2,000 workers on the power project. Some won't be back at work on Monday—winter is approaching.

"We have our snowbirds," Worrall says. "They work only during the summer. At the first cold snap, they're gone." There's another reason for the high rate of turnover in the work force. It's called the

"Gillette Syndrome" (Gillette being another Wyoming town prospering on coal), whereby the wife of a worker rebels at the boredom of life in a trailer. The husband must choose: his wife or his job. Love and devotion have something to do with the decision, and so has the peregrine nature of the average worker at the plant. They leave.

It is best to leave Rock Springs in the thin light of early morning, when the town is free of its feverishness. It will be two hours before the carpenters arrive to erect yet another portable classroom at an overcrowded school. At the power plant, the trucks that carry the coal are at rest on their $4,000 tires. Chairs are stacked on the tables in bars where nightlights raise altars of bottles above the darkness.

At such times, Rock Springs seems swallowed up in the stunning spaciousness of Wyoming. A statistic comes alive: There are fewer than four people for each of the 97,203 square miles in the state. For many, this isolation is the greatest of all the blessings bestowed on those who live in the Rocky Mountain states. Let others, they say, submit themselves to the torturous restriction of two square feet on a New York subway during rush hour.

And yet, Rock Springs *did* happen. Will there not be more and more Rock Springs as designs on the wealth of the region grow bolder? Most of the coal, oil shale, and uranium in the country are in the West, and on federal land. And the powerful weight of the federal government is behind development of these resources.

Regional planners in western Colorado have concluded: "We should learn from our mistakes. . . . We should not have to repeat the errors of Gillette or Rock Springs."

Richard D. Lamm, Colorado's young (39 when elected in 1974) governor, has warned: "We won't become the nation's slag heap."

Governor Thomas Judge of Montana has demanded a major role for his state in decision-making at the federal level. "I'd like the final say . . . [as to] where mining should and shouldn't take place," he told officials of the Department of the Interior.

As experienced politicians, however, both Lamm and Judge are aware of the futility of confrontation with the federal government on a state-by-state basis.

"We have a tenuous line to walk between confrontation and articulating our concerns to them [the federal government]," Lamm said at a meeting of Western governors. "Unless we combine regionally, we're going to be run down."

Of all the Rocky Mountain states, only one—Colorado—has locally owned industrial capital to any substantial degree. In the six-state region of New Mexico, Colorado, Wyoming, Utah, Idaho, and Montana, the bank deposits totaled less than 20 billion dollars in December 1974. (In Florida alone they were 24 billion; in Texas, 42 billion; in California, 79 billion.) Separately, the states have relationships with Washington not too far removed from those of colony and crown; acting in consort, they take on clout. Thus, there have come into being the Federation of Rocky Mountain States, and the Western Governors' Regional Energy Policy Office. In many ways, now, state boundaries in the Rocky Mountains are but lines on a map.

"Our purpose," an official of the Federation told me, "is to develop policies not for any single state, but for the entire region. Together, we make up a large segment of the country. We comprise, in effect, an underdeveloped country in the middle of the most developed country in the world.''

Driving north from Rock Springs, I couldn't help feeling that economic hardships weigh lightly on this land. There is a blank check of scenery to be filled in and cashed for the viewing. It was late enough in the year for the newborn magpies to have left the nest, but here and there blooms remained on the Indian paintbrush. The bracts surrounding the tubular flowers were like shucks of fire. There's thievery beneath this scarlet innocence, however, for the Indian paintbrush is part parasite. It pushes its roots through the soil in search of the roots of another plant, and when contact is made, it diverts part of the host plant's food to its own use.

The route I took is along stations of history. Ahead was South Pass, the gate in the Rockies through which those who sought the new land in California and Oregon passed more than a century ago. They came through here from St. Louis and Kentucky, from Maine and the tidewater flats of Virginia. They came to South Pass because it offered the easiest passage across the mountains.

I T'S WORTHWHILE to take the time and pause here briefly, to walk where the wagons rolled, and imagine for a moment that you can hear the groan of leather, and a piece of whippish birch zinging on the dusty rump of an ox, and the lamentations of a woman brought to widowhood by an Indian's arrow.

To the north is the Wind River Range of the Rockies, and Shoshone Indian land. Land, too, where the mountain men trappers brought their crustiness to bear in conquering the wilderness. Among these men, whose contributions to the settlement of the West have often been overlooked, was Jim Bridger. He was illiterate—unable to write his own name—but he discovered the Great Salt Lake in 1824. He was an early explorer of Yellowstone, and it was he who blazed the routes to be later followed by the Overland Stage, the Pony Express, and the Union Pacific Railroad with its push to Promontory, Utah.

Bridger's name is frequently encountered in the mountains today. It's been given to a national wilderness area and a waterfall, a fort and a ferry, a town, a lake, and a peak. Indeed, most of the activity at Rock Springs centers on the Jim Bridger Steam Electric Project.

As a trapper, Bridger roamed throughout the mountains in search of beaver. It was this pursuit of the valuable pelts that led to the exploration of much of the wilderness. In addition, a glandular secretion of the animal, castoreum, was marketable as a medicine for a variety of ailments. So they came, Jim Bridger and others, with their traps, following the wooded streams in alpine meadows, ever watchful for stick dams and shavings at the base of a tree. In a good year, it was not impossible for a trapper to earn as much as $25,000.

Trappers gathered once a year to sell their pelts and take on new supplies. It was a time, too, for drinking, fighting, gambling, and encounters with squaws. This was the rendezvous. Alone in the wilderness as winter moved through like the running of bulls, a trapper might feel the presence of death, but thoughts of the coming gathering stoked his determination to survive.

There is in Wyoming a town called Daniel, population 125. Nearby is the site of the 1835 rendezvous, fabled in the fur trade for the attendance of Jim Bridger and Kit Carson. They camped there, on the Green River, along with several thousand Indians—Utes, Snakes, Nez Perces, Flatheads—and scores of trappers. Whiskey was going for five dollars a pint.

Tradition tells of the presence at this rendezvous of a drunken bully known as Shunar, eager to gratify his lust for a comely Arapaho Indian girl. Kit Carson also had designs on the girl. Shunar was mean (the bully as coward in Western lore is fiction; there was usually lots of muscle to backstop the braying). The two men dueled with pistols. Shunar lost the fight; some say he lost his life. And Carson, a giant among this nation's frontiersmen though he stood only five feet, four inches, took the Arapaho girl for his wife. Her name was Waa-nibe, which means Grass Singing; and it was among her people, wrote a historian of the mountain men, that Kit Carson found "his first experience of an ordered society."

While Carson was fighting his duel, a doctor attending the rendezvous was removing an arrowhead that had been embedded in Jim Bridger's back for three years.

When he was old and in poor health, Jim Bridger went back east to Missouri. He was nearly blind. Stanley Vestal, Bridger's biographer, quotes the old scout as saying, "I wish I war back thar among the mountains agin. A man kin see so much farther in that country."

Yes, there are visions to be had in the Rockies unlike any others on earth: of a sky so broad and far-reaching as to deflate the bloat of human arrogance; of high meadows hung like heroic frescoes; of ravens and grizzlies taking kills in the natural order of things. And of a desolate stretch of chalky mesas where junipers are shaped by the wind—oil shale country.

Some say that the boom in oil shale is near. Others were saying the same thing more than half-a-century ago. Read the words of the NATIONAL GEOGRAPHIC in a story published in 1918: "As the great Creator, through His servants of old, caused water to flow from the rock in the wilderness, so through twentieth century science, He is causing oil, for ages locked up in the shales of America, to be released for the relief of human necessity."

No, He wasn't—not then, and not now. The oil is there, all right, the equivalent of about 1.8 trillion barrels of it spread over a 17,000-square-mile area touching on Colorado, Utah, and Wyoming, with the richest deposits in the Piceance Creek Basin of Colorado.

Experts estimate that about 600 billion barrels of oil could be reclaimed from the shale—enough to meet the needs of the whole country for a hundred years. Why, then, is it sitting there, compressed in the shale like flavoring in hard rock candy?

Oil shale had its beginnings in the salty lakes that covered great reaches of the West about fifty million years ago. In the course of eight or nine million years, algae and insects and other small aquatic creatures would die and their remains would sift down into lake-floor mud. Eventually the mud, laced with organic matter, solidified into stone. This organic matter is called kerogen.

Heated to about 900° F., some of the kerogen will melt; with the temperature raised even higher, gases will form. It is the condensation of these vapors that yields a usable crude oil. To produce 35,000 barrels of oil a day, a plant would have to process 50,000 tons of broken-up rock, leaving mountains of spent shale to be disposed of. (Even if artificially compacted, spent shale has a volume at least 15 percent greater than the original rock had.) Engineers have tried for years to find a way to recover oil in situ—that is, without having to mine the rock. To date, only one method looks at all promising.

As these particulars indicate, it's expensive business to recover shale oil. The technology has not been perfected. There are environmental problems. Moreover, title to some of the richest shale is clouded; one analyst assumes that "shale ownership cases will be argued in court by lawyers not yet born...." Private companies are, understandably, reluctant to proceed with development unless assured that the federal government will cover possible financial losses.

Eighty percent of oil shale land in the West is federally owned, so, once again, the states must shout to be heard. Often, the voice is shrill, saying, in effect, leave the shale alone. At other times it is con-

In an 1865 gold rush, supply wagons clog the main street of "Last Chance Gulch"—now a prized historic area in Helena, Montana's capital.

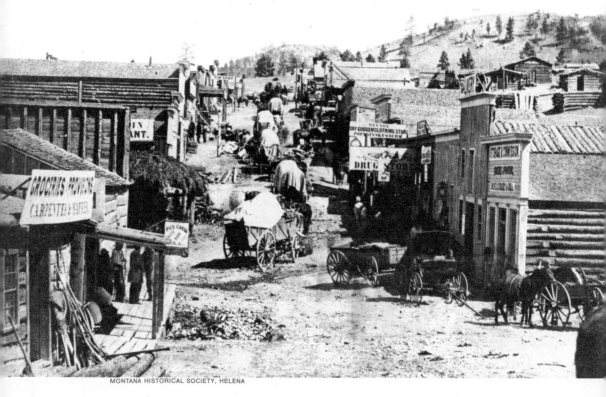

ciliatory, calling for development along state-directed lines. Sometimes it allows for the uncertainties of the future. Governor Calvin Rampton of Utah has recommended a 50,000-barrel-a-day development—but warned that Utah should do "everything in its power" to stop it, if it endangered "our clean air and our sparkling streams."

Today there are experimental shale projects, just as there were in 1918; but small-scale pilot developments are much easier than "scaled-up" profit-making ones. Now, as then, it takes a great deal of energy to process the shale. It takes massive amounts of water as well; and water has long been at a premium in the Mountain West. In truth, large-scale commercial production of shale oil can hardly be expected before the year 2000.

N̲o TOWN has stood longer on the threshold of prosperity from oil shale than Rifle, Colorado. Periodically, since 1903, Rifle has geared itself for the boom. It has yet to come. With the opening of an experimental plant in the area, there has been a flurry of recent activity but, essentially, Rifle remains a quiet town where the vacuum cleaner working the frayed carpet in the lobby of the Winchester Hotel can be heard a block away.

Robert W. Wamsley, who works for the Chamber of Commerce, is optimistic. "We've had to hire additional teachers," he says. "Bank deposits have increased, and real estate prices have become unreal. Land here that went for $200, $300 an acre a few years ago now sells for as much as $10,000 an acre." But when a man called from halfway across the country to say that he was selling everything and coming to Rifle to work, Wamsley had to discourage him.

The jobs just don't exist. Until they do, Rifle will have to ride on the fame it achieved in 1972 when "World Artist Christo" unfurled his latest work there. Called the "Valley Curtain," it was 8,000 pounds of bright-orange nylon cloth that had cost something like $700,000. Christo placed the curtain so that it spanned a quarter-mile gap in the Grand Hogback, six miles northeast of town, and there it hung until the wind shredded it, billowing and shining and leaving the good folks of Rifle to ponder the meaning and uses of modern art.

Oil shale held little attraction for the armies of prospectors who converged on the Mountain West in the last half of the 19th century. The lure was gold and silver and copper—all there for the taking.

The gold is there, 'most anywhere,
You can take it out rich with an iron crowbar,
And where it is thick, with a shovel and pick,
You can pick it out in lumps as big as a brick.
Then ho boys ho, to Pikes Peak we'll go....

As late as 1900, there were more than 50,000 miners working claims in the area around Cripple Creek, Colorado (in 1974, a clerk in the Cripple Creek courthouse came across 11 bags of dust and ore in a vault; county commissioners sensed a bonanza, but, alas, the stash assayed out at $27.05). Northern Idaho's incredibly beautiful Coeur d'Alene district was found to hold vast deposits of silver and lead. In Montana, a hill called Butte would be opened and worked for billions of dollars' worth of copper.

Butte deserves better than its reputation as the Siberia of the New World. If lacking in charm, the town abounds in character. Shacky wooden houses press in on a downtown where such establishments as the "Pekin Noodle Parlor" conduct business. Stale odors gust out of bars where some of the most memorable brawls in the West were staged. Also, Butte counts among its residents one Evel Knievel, most daring of all daredevils. In 1974 his unsuccessful attempt to vault the Snake River Canyon on his Sky-Cycle X-2—a steam-powered cross between a motorcycle and a rocket ship—gave millions of television watchers a sense of the scale of things in the Rockies: From rim to rim the canyon under him measured 1,765 feet; from rim to river, 540 feet.

Butte's outstanding feature is a gigantic hole called the Berkeley Pit. There, the Anaconda Company takes 290,000 tons of material each day, of which 45,000 tons are copper-bearing ore. Production began in 1955, and now the pit is 6,000 feet across and 1,200 feet deep. The work is expected to continue for another 15 or 20 years. Even now the great chasm has reached the eastern fringe of Butte, and there's talk of developing a new business district on the south side of town.

Anaconda once commanded great power in Montana. It owned almost all of the major newspapers. It could—and did—control elections. Bill Christiansen, lieutenant governor of Montana, recalls the power of the copper company: "When I was in the legislature, there was a standing joke about reapportionment. They'd say that of the new 50-member Senate, 49 would be appointed by Anaconda, and one would run at large."

OF ALL THE ROCKY MOUNTAIN STATES, none is more protective of the environment than Montana. The state has what is perhaps the strongest reclamation act in the country. It also has a coal conservation act that, in effect, allows the state to tell a company how to operate its mines. Bill Christiansen has been a leading force in getting such legislation on the books.

"The copper industry so dominated the whole economic and political scene in Montana that I think it alerted people not to let the coal companies do the same thing," he says. "I really think that was a blessing in disguise—a lesson in disguise, if you will. And, you know, you talk about the tail wagging the dog and so forth, but those companies become extremely powerful in a rather short time, and if you don't hit the issue head on, before long you're picking away at the edges. I think we have a climate here that the coal companies can live with, but I'm glad that the climate was developed by Montana, and not the coal companies."

The copper reserves in Montana and Utah remain extensive, as do those of lead and silver in Idaho and Colorado. And there is gold still—David Mosch will tell you that.

David is 15 years old now. He lives with his mother and father and two sisters in a house that sits against the wall of a cliff in Idaho Springs, Colorado, not far from Denver. His father, Alvin, is a hard-rock miner who on one occasion, while prospecting for uranium in Utah, had men come seeking his claim and order him at gunpoint to dig his own grave. "I didn't know at the time if they were kidding or not," he says, smiling weakly, "but I dug." Alvin's father was also a hard-rock miner, and so was his grandfather, who walked all the way to Colorado from New York.

In 1969 David's mother, Patricia, became the first woman to graduate from the Colorado School of Mines with two degrees at once: one in geological and one in mining engineering.

It is little wonder, then, that when the Mosch family goes on an outing, they pack shovel and pick, and head for one of the couple of hundred old mining claims that Alvin has bought up. "We bought these claims when gold was selling for $35 an ounce," he says, "and we hung on to them with the certainty that the price would go way up." And so it has—to more than $100 an ounce.

On the Labor Day weekend of 1974, the family was at a claim site when David appeared to announce that he had made an important find. "I didn't believe him at first," Alvin recalls, "but when the assay report came back, I decided I had better take a look."

What 14-year-old David Mosch found was a large vein of gold and silver. Its value has not been determined, but could easily run well beyond a million.

The find will set off no new stampede of fortune-seekers to what an observer of the 19th-century gold rushes referred to as "the auriferous arteries that were engorged with a golden current by the Fire Heart of an age that now sleeps with the forgotten centuries." In the first place, the prospector would be required to file an environmental impact statement before retrieving his riches, and the thought of doing that can sap the will of the strongest of men.

Protection of the environment involves the filing of reports, of petitions and petitions against the petitions, of court hearings and long waits for action by appropriate agencies. It is a fallacy that such measures raise the unemployment figures. Indeed, Senator Floyd Haskell of Colorado has predicted, in a speech to the National Wildlife Federation, that more people will be working as a result of environmental protection programs than would be without them.

Still, there are those who lose their jobs and those who are caught in the middle, who suddenly feel the pressure for adherence to the new codes for use of the land getting so heavy that there is hardly room for breathing. Percy D. Gray is such a person.

Percy Gray is manager of the only matchstick factory west of the Mississippi—at Mancos, Colorado. At the small plant he runs for the Ohio Match Company, they make the sticks out of aspen wood, the same quaking aspen that stands, in my mind, as among the most noble of trees. Thirty-two persons work at the plant, and about a third of those are of ethnic minorities—Indians, Mexicans, and others. There are few places to work in Mancos, and those who find jobs at the plant tend to stay on for a long time.

It's a cold fall morning, and Percy Gray is standing in the yard of the plant, waiting for a load of aspen logs to arrive. He pulls the zipper up on his jacket and says:

"We're having our environmental problems. We now have to bring in some wood that's of no use to us whatsoever in order to clean up the logging area. I suppose it's the right thing to do, but I'm telling you, it complicates things."

The mountains are all around us, and Gray points to one, saying, "When this plant started 27 years ago, they brought in some Swedes from Minnesota to cut the aspen on that mountain. That gray area — see it? — is all aspen, a regrowth of what the Swedes cut, with handsaws, 27 years ago. Now it's ready for cutting again.

"Lord, how things have changed. Take the boilers we have here in the plant. When we put them in back in 1946, no one said anything about the smoke coming out of the stacks. But now I've been given a citation by the Environmental Protection Agency, and we only burn wood scraps."

Percy Gray never raises his voice, never displays anger, and his concerns for the future are genuine. He understands the need for protecting the land, and he supports those efforts, but he feels unfairly put upon to have to buy wood that he can't use, and to pay a fine for putting some woodfire smoke in the air. What is more natural to the environment than a wood fire? So he has to cut a few corners, such as making the matchsticks one-sixteenth of an inch shorter.

"After all," he rationalizes, "the matchstick is a lever, and by making it shorter, we make it stronger." As it is now, each of the 52 million sticks turned out every eight hours will support six pounds. These are kitchen matches, the big ones you can crack to flame with a skillful scratch of a fingernail.

Well, chances are that Percy D. Gray and his close friends at the Mancos matchstick factory will still be on the job for years to come. He'll do something about that smoke, and he'll find a way to utilize that scrap aspen.

And tomorrow morning, when he's back out in the yard, waiting for another load of logs, he'll look to the regrowth area on the distant mountain and wonder again how those Swedes from Minnesota managed to cut all those trees using nothing but handsaws.

Power lines channel thousands of kilowatts as far as 800 miles to the Northwest Coast from the coal-burning Jim Bridger Steam Electric Project in Sweetwater County, Wyoming. Such projects, fueled by strip mines, give rise to growing concern for protection of the environment.

Petroleum from the Rocky Mountains: The region poured more than 250 million barrels into the nation's three-billion-barrel production for 1974. Roughneck Rick Oakes (opposite) shoulders a 30-foot length of casing pipe for a new flowing well in the Blue Bell Oil Field in Utah. Once the spontaneous flow slows down, pumps like the rig at left raise the crude—which goes by pipeline or truck to refineries. A Chevron refinery in Salt Lake City (below) processes 45,000 barrels of crude daily for gasoline, aviation and industrial fuels, heating oil, coke, and liquid petroleum gases.

*D*awn of a clear day—a rarity at Denver in recent years—reveals the Front Range on the
skyline as Colorado's capital braces for smog from freeway traffic. A proposed subway

system may lessen pollution. Formerly a gold camp, Denver leads the mountain states as a financial and cultural hub—and it ranks as a major center for research in respiratory diseases.

*N*ew Wyoming residents bring to life the ghost
town of Superior, its population now quadrupled to
475. Bridal couple, Teresa and Robert Townsend (in a
top hat) entertain wedding guests in Superior's Palace
Bar—where a pool player continues his free-wheeling
game. At the nearby town of Reliance, a trailer court
set up by the Bridger Project houses the construction
workers who will soon move on.

*S*now speckles a coalbed laid bare by a dragline crane that strips off tons of overburden near

Rock Springs, Wyoming. The Jim Bridger Project promises to restore the miles of open cut.

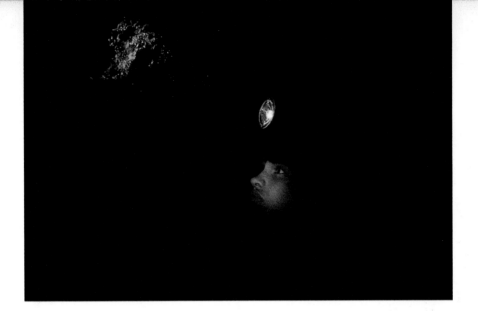

Securing a ceiling against rock falls, miner Fred Castle drills bolt holes to attach steel plates. The Idarado Mining Company owns this vein; its hard-rock ores of lead, zinc, and copper sparkle with water sprayed to reduce dust. Superstition barriers against women underground have begun to crumble: Karen Nurnberg, who shed her safety glasses for a portrait, runs a passenger and supply elevator. To offset declining prices of copper, lead, and zinc, the Colorado company now reworks old gold and silver mines. While inspecting an inactive claim owned by his family, teen-age David Mosch discovered a gold, silver, and lead vein possibly worth several million dollars.

*O*n *Coeur d'Alene Lake in Idaho, a logger prods cedar toward a sawmill of the Potlatch Corporation. Demand for wood and wood products rises, at home and abroad. In the ever-shrinking wilderness of the American Rockies, public lands provided more than 70 percent of the regional timber harvest for 1970. Below, timbermen of the Champion International Corporation attach a sky-line cable to a ponderosa pine; like a ski lift, their hoist pulls trees to the top of the Montana slope. Timber's natural enemy, fire can consume acres within minutes as soaring brands from burning trees spread the blaze. At the Northern Forestry Department in Missoula, Montana, tests using one-inch-by-five-inch dowels help determine how fast a fire can move in still air (left) or controlled speeds of wind up to 25 miles per hour.*

*F*ueling a backfire, a professional firefighter helps check a blaze that claimed
nearly 4,500 acres of aspen, spruce, and pine near Burn, Colorado, in 1975.
He wears an asbestos jacket, a specially designed pack, and a bandanna over
his nose and mouth. After ten hours of felling trees and bulldozing fire lines
ten yards wide, an exhausted crew files silently back to camp for a meal
of hamburger steaks. Careless elk hunters touched off the four-day fire,
the most destructive on record for the state. It ruined recreation and water-
shed areas, wildlife forage, and timber, valued overall at $6,600,000.

CHAPTER THREE

A Sense of Freedom: Sports in the Rockies

HEY ARE ALL OVER these magnificent mountains, schussing and poling and stirring the powder to a fare-thee-well. They come from nearby and faraway, by car and plane, train and bus. They come, like birds to a flyway, to put themselves on paths of flight and let the dagger-like air of winter cut into their faces.

They come, yes, to ski.

President Gerald Ford is among them. So are stars of industry and show business. The biggest names are in attendance at Aspen and Vail and Sun Valley, but the ski industry in the Rockies extends far beyond that. There are scores of resorts and some expanding. Indeed, skiing is the mother lode of a recreational bonanza.

Prior to World War II, recreation as a business had little economic impact on the region. Yellowstone drew visitors, as it has since its founding as the nation's first national park more than a century ago, and the Union Pacific Railroad hauled dowagers and others of high social rank to its plush resort of Sun Valley. For the most part, however, the mountains and forests remained locked in isolation.

Aspen was a drowsy relic of an era when millions of dollars' worth of ore was taken from the ground there. It was a town built on silver, and not much thought was given to the white gold that lay in great depths on the surrounding mountains. It would be years before Aspen would become established as a major resort, offering possibly the finest skiing in all the world.

In the early 1940's, servicemen were sent to the Rockies for training. Later, when the fighting ended, many would return to the mountains as they had vowed to do. They came back to live and work and renew a love for the land where lithe, tawny cougars still roam. Veterans of the 10th Mountain Division returned to develop recreational skiing as a premier attraction for visitors.

Blind pioneer of programs for the handicapped in Norway, Erling Stordahl
finishes a cross-country event near Frisco, Colorado. Nearly 60 blind
skiers, each with a guide, savored the bite of the wind and the scent of pines.

This was a unique fighting unit of volunteers. Members of the 10th trained in the high country of Colorado. Camp Hale was a hundred miles from Denver, at an elevation of 9,200 feet. It was no place for the weak. A training maneuver might mean an overnight march on skis in temperatures of 20 and 30 below.

On weekends and other off-duty times, some members of the division skied the single run at Aspen. And then they went off to Italy to fight the Germans. When the war ended, there were returning members of the 10th who remembered how well skis ran in the dry, fluffy powder; it was they who played a major role in the establishment of skiing as a major industry in the Rockies.

That was in the 1940's. By 1975, Idaho had 26 established ski areas. Colorado had 31. Utah, New Mexico, and Montana were active, too. In British Columbia, experienced skiers were finding what many consider to be the ultimate experience in winter sports — riding a helicopter into the Purcell Mountains for a run as long as ten miles or a vertical drop as great as 8,700 feet.

Devotees of heli-skiing argue the merits of their favorite areas with happy doggedness. They are split, fairly evenly, into partisans of the Cariboos, the Monashees, and the Bugaboos in the Purcell range — areas limited by the range of the helicopters to roughly a thousand square miles maximum apiece.

A native of Aspen sketches the appeal of the Bugaboos, where particular runs bear names as expressive as Ambrosia, Wildcat, and Gazoom: "Granite spires overhead, glaciers underfoot — except crossing a crevasse, when nothing is underfoot but fear." One expert heeded the guide's warning to stop above him — but even as she swirled to a stop, her pole jabbed through the snow to blue-black emptiness. Gingerly, with intense coaching by the guide, she inched away from the crevasse to secure footing. Rarely does the danger of glacier skiing mar the exhilaration of fine powder free from crowds.

Aspen itself had only 700 year-round residents at the end of World War II. The population is now about 2,400. In addition, 250,000 visitors crowd into the town each winter, most of them to take to the 300 miles of trails set aside for skiing. Sun Valley, meanwhile, welcomed the masses without scorning the upper classes. Condominium developments went up in the shadow of Baldy Mountain, and now the rises of masonry and glass are in view from the room where Ernest Hemingway wrote parts of *For Whom the Bell Tolls.*

In Montana, the late Chet Huntley of television newscasting fame pushed for development of a sprawling, 10,647-acre ski resort called Big Sky. The project encountered opposition from ranchers and others in the area, just north of Yellowstone, but it finally opened in 1973. With the success of the venture long in doubt, it may be that Big Sky foreshadows development overkill. More and more voices are rising in opposition to the opening of new resorts.

The loudest voices are heard in Colorado, and one of them belongs to Dick Lamm. It was he who, in 1972, took a key role in opposing the use of the Denver area as the site for the 1976 Winter Olympics. A vote was held on the question of funding, and the result was 514,228 to 350,964 — with the majority endorsing Lamm's position.

Innsbruck, Austria, won the Olympics, and Dick Lamm went on to win the governorship of Colorado in 1974.

The great surge of recreational activity in the Rockies was certain to occur. The offerings there, for both winter and summer fun, are numerous and outstanding. The mountain states hold America's crown jewels of wilderness, including such national parks as Glacier, Rocky Mountain, Grand Teton, Yellowstone, and, in Canada, Banff and Jasper. The region is a magnet for campers and hikers. It is the great escape from urban ills, a place for putting thoughts in order. . . .

On a February morning, when the Tetons hovered over the valley like stern monitors of silence, I clasped on a pair of cross-country skis, and went into the forest. There were no packed trails to follow — only the shadowy maze of corridors through the pines. The snow squeaked under the waxed push of the laminated wood. Strength surged through my spirit until I wanted to bellow. In fact I did bellow: I raised my voice and hurled it away, and listened as it caromed off the trees and hills. It seemed the thing to do, just as it seemed right to fantasize about my ability to accomplish any feat once I emerged from the forest. I could solve the Middle East crisis, and run the mile in less than three minutes. I could learn to play the French horn, and work the Sunday crossword without a dictionary.

NOWHERE ELSE IN THE NATION, I believe, is the drug of wilderness solitude as strong as it is in the Rockies. That is why songs are written about these mountains — why a woman named Katharine Lee Bates could look out from the heights of Pikes Peak and be inspired to put words on paper that began "O beautiful for spacious skies." And why another woman, Maryhale Woolsey, could give the world a song that has endured, no matter how lacking in genius of words and melody — that being, of course, "When It's Springtime In the Rockies." Men bellow in the mountains, women compose . . . but then there's John Denver, Aspen-based balladeer whose songs of rejoicing in the mountains have spilled out to the nation like a flood of chocolate-malt milkshakes.

Skiing at the well-known resorts in the Rockies often involves long waits at the lifts. Fees are high — $700 for a season lift pass at Aspen in 1974-1975. But rarely is there inadequate snow.

"We get an average of 300 inches of fine powder snow a year," Roger Rountree said as we looked out on hundreds of acres of groomed ski terrain masking the face of a mountain. "If it rains in Los Angeles, we know that will be followed by a snowstorm here."

Rountree is an official of the Purgatory Ski Resort, in the San Juan Mountains, about 25 miles from Durango, Colorado. Since its opening in 1965, the resort has steadily gained popularity among experienced skiers in the Mountain West.

Snow comes early to Purgatory. The season usually starts about Thanksgiving and runs until Easter. During that time Purgatory averages 700 skiers on a weekday, more than twice as many on a Saturday or Sunday. Among those who challenge runs with such names as Angel's Tread and Divine Comedy are persons without sight.

"We have had a program to teach the blind to ski for the past three years," Rountree told me. "It started when a blind girl from Houston named Diana Alexander told us she wanted to learn."

Diana and an instructor went to the top of a mountain, and, with each holding the end of a bamboo pole, they descended, making turns together as the instructor gave verbal guidance. Soon, Diana was racing down the slope with the instructor at her side describing the terrain. She quickly learned to ski, and now there are programs for the blind on many of the mountains.

According to Erling Stordahl of Norway, who went blind at age 12, "We all stumble around in the dark. . . ." Some are literally blind, some "haven't learned to see with their thoughts," and "therefore we need each other." He brought his philosophy of sports for the handicapped to Frisco, Colorado, in 1975 for an international "Race for Light." The Sons of Norway Foundation lent support; King Olav V sent greetings. Trails were tamped down side by side — a track for the sighted guide, one for the blind contestant — and skiers from the United States, Canada, Norway, and Uganda made their way four miles along the course. Stordahl summed up the elation of it: "The track is our sight. The skis feel the way. . . . We suddenly are physically and mentally free."

Fritz Tatzer, ski school director at Purgatory, told me why the blind so often learn to ski faster than sighted persons: "They listen to everything you say and then do it. Also, since they can't see the steepness of the slopes, they don't fear them."

I know what he means. It's still a puzzle to me why I was up there, on the summit of a mountain that wears clouds like a bib. I don't ski well at all, but if I was ever going to get down from that windy, frozen station, it would have to be on skis. Of course, I could have taken the lift and claimed my trick knee was acting up. But I pushed off and was gone — fast as a log on a skid and just as prone.

Undaunted by the cumbersome attire fashionable in 1910, enthusiasts in Colorado's Rockies spend pleasant hours skiing — now a major sport in the area.

Few mountains offer more of a challenge to skiers than Rendez-vous, near Jackson Hole, Wyoming. It is a mountain tormented by the harshest of winter weather, a mountain lashed by blizzards and obscured by whiteouts. When the weather is clear, the sight from the top is jarring. The vertical drop is 4,500 feet, and the longest groomed run goes for four and a half miles.

But that's why many come to the Rockies for recreation—the challenge. Often, in winter, it is a challenge even to get to the resorts. Many of the smaller airports are closed as often as not, because of poor visibility. In Grand Teton National Park, where the airport serving Jackson is located, the grinding of motors is a familiar sound as prop planes on scheduled runs circle the area waiting for a break in the weather. Few regular visitors have not heard these words from the workaday vocabulary of pilots on the run: "Sorry, ladies and gentlemen, but we'll have to continue on to Idaho Falls."

Road travel is unpredictable. Highways must cross mountain passes, and if snow piles up deep enough to cover a semi-trailer truck, there is nothing to do but turn around. Of 34 passes in Colorado, 4 are closed throughout the winter; among them is 12,093-foot-high Independence Pass on the eastern approach to Aspen.

The State of Colorado is responsible for maintaining 9,200 miles of highway. For eight months of the year it is a formidable task, including work to combat the most fearsome of winter's blows in the Rockies—the avalanche.

These killer cargoes of moving snow have claimed at least 48 lives in Colorado during the past 25 years. Risk has increased with the growing popularity of cross-country skiing. Ski touring often leads to the back country where the makeup of the terrain under the snow is unknown, and where the weight of one skier might fracture the powder and set off a massive slide. So it is, too, with mountain climbing in the winter.

For example, in January of 1974, a 15-member party set out for a two-week climbing-ski touring trek in the Tetons. It was snowing heavily; one night there were gusty winds estimated at 75 miles per hour. Finally, the weather cleared, and the group approached the Teton Glacier. To reach it, they had to climb a moraine, an accumulation of earth and stone left by the moving glacier. The second person in the procession over the moraine was 50 feet from the top when the avalanche occurred. Three of the climbers died.

Clambering along the moraine had dislodged a hard slab of snow 350 yards wide. A report on the tragedy concluded that "the party ascended the wrong slope at the wrong time."

Yet they were led by experienced climbers. Those with less experience are forever being hauled down from the heights, and the number of reported accidents has increased sharply in the 1970's.

"It used to be that going to the mountains was only a fair-weather pastime, and only for the stouthearted," said Dave Moore of Evergreen, Colorado. "Now, with more leisure time and more money to spend, recreation in the mountains is a year-round activity. They come out here with the time, the money, and the equipment. What they don't have is the experience."

Moore is a former president of the International Mountain Rescue Association. His interest began more than 20 years ago when a high school friend disappeared while hiking in Rocky Mountain National Park. "In those days only park rangers conducted search and rescue in the parks," he said. "They didn't find a trace of my friend." Now there are 285 search and rescue groups in Colorado, ranging from sheriffs' posses to units specializing in mountain work.

As a member of a rescue group since 1959, Dave Moore has participated in scores of missions over the years. Education, he feels, is the key to reducing the number of emergencies. Thus, he works with youth groups to drive home the importance of proper preparation for challenging the mountains.

DEATH BY AVALANCHE — the "white death" — comes to those, too, who are in the mountains not for recreation but simply on their way from one place to another. For a motorist, the tragedy occurs when the slide sweeps across a highway with a force of, say, 35 tons per square yard of snow, or enough to lift a car (a truck, even) and hurl it into space. Short of keeping the highway closed all winter, the most effective preventive measure is to set the avalanche off under controlled conditions.

Wyoming State Highway 22 is lifted to an elevation of 8,431 feet as it crosses Teton Pass. It is a good road kept in good repair. But on a Friday in February there were barriers on both sides of 22 where it starts its climb to the pass. The risk of an avalanche from "Glory Bowl," a depression high on a mountain with a notorious chute-like slide below it, was too great to permit traffic. The snow had to be shaken loose and allowed to come down under supervision. A state highway crew from Jackson was about to attempt that by firing the shells of a 105-millimeter recoilless rifle into the snow pack.

"Shooting to start an avalanche is a good guess and a be-damned." Bruce Petersen was talking as he twirled wheels to position the large weapon. We would be shooting across a gorge, at a range of about 3,000 yards from Glory Bowl. The first of the shells, 40.8 inches long, was brought up and pushed into the chamber.

Fog rolled across the gorge, obscuring the target. "We'll just have to wait if you want to see it," Petersen said. More than 25 inches of snow had fallen in the area in the past four days, and now the land lay still and white with all its voices smothered under the wind-furrowed covering that reached to the throats of young pines.

The fog cleared, and seconds after the firing a puff of black smoke rose from the target area. We waited for the snow to start moving. But that didn't happen. Except for an outbreak of ripples that ran as slow and soft as tears, the snow held to the bowl. Another shell was fired, and still the avalanche failed to kick off. In all we lobbed seven shells at the mountain that morning without success.

"It just goes to show you that there's no such thing as an avalanche expert," a member of the highway crew said. "Avalanche control is nothing more than alchemy."

I looked over the terrain through field glasses and saw a golden eagle in flight. He was getting close to the crossarm of power lines.

If he landed there, he could die of electrocution. He turned, however, and went off the other way. Between power lines, artillery shells ripping the air, and lumbermen chopping down all the best perches, it's not easy for a bird these days.

Glory Bowl remained packed and dangerous, and Highway 22 remained closed until a week later when the snow departed that mountain in a spectacular push to the gorge below.

It was because of closed roads, avalanche conditions, and other aspects of what is known in the Mountain West as "a tight winter" that some cold-weather recreational activities became popular. For example, with nothing else to do, men began to race sleds pulled by horses. That activity, sometimes called chariot racing, continues today. Since 1972 the Jackson Hole Shrine Club has sponsored "invitational cutter races" to raise funds for a crippled children's hospital in Salt Lake City. In the 1930's the town's races were purely for fun; the course was Broadway, which runs through the middle of town, and fans could visit the nearest saloon between events.

Without recreation to ease the tensions of winter, residents of small towns in the mountains often tend to become testy. They start to carp at one another. Such was the case in one town where I spent several days. A letter appeared in the local newspaper expressing criticism of the teaching of karate in the junior high school. The writer was a woman, and in the next issue of the paper she was attacked by a student of the martial arts for her "tendency to shoot her mouth off about things she knows nothing about." More letters followed, and before long the issue had been expanded to include discussion of the morals of a fellow citizen.

By spring, however, when the avalanche lily was starting to flower, all had been forgiven and forgotten.

It has come to pass in our time that the quest for new lifestyles has reached out to nature. Teenagers with acne problems, housewives sapped of spirit through years of kitchen drudgery, and businessmen gone fat and flat at the desk are among those who are trekking through the Rockies in search of revitalization.

Some come as enrollees in "survival training" courses. They are sent packing into the wilderness on foot, in summer or winter, and most emerge with a second wind of life pulsing through their bodies. They return to their urban haunts wearing the glow of the experience like the tan of a vacation at the beach.

Others come to the Mountain West for stays at dude ranches. There, they dress in jeans and boots, and raise their voices in song around campfires. They live out the dream of many Americans—to play cowboy for a week or two and let the cares of home and office be trampled under the hoofs of their mounts. They pay to participate in ranching chores, and are happy for it.

And, of course, they come to visit the national parks.

It was more than a century ago that Jim Bridger told of seeing wondrous things in a region of the Rockies—things such as a column of water as thick as his body spouting 60 feet in the air. He was called a liar. He told of seeing pools of steaming water, and fields of mud that bubbled up and popped. Liar, they said.

Bridger had seen all that, for he had come across the land that would later take the name of Yellowstone and become the doyen of national parks not only in this country, but, indeed, in all the world.

Of all its marvels, one stands alone. I first saw it about five years ago, and at that time I wrote: "As the tower of hot water surged out of the earth, I looked around and saw wonder reflected in nearly every face." An elderly couple next to me held hands, as if the hissing waters were pronouncing a benediction of happiness and good health for their late years. "Yet I only heard one voice — a rasping whisper urging the geyser to 'Go, boy, go.'"

Old Faithful continues to work its magic for the crowds, erupting once every 65 minutes or so. What visitors miss these days are the roadside black bears. By 1971 the Park Service had closed its last open-pit garbage dumps and installed bearproof garbage cans, to keep both blacks and grizzlies from dependence on "artificial" food. The scroungers and the roadside beggars, say the authorities, have disappeared to the back country to fend for themselves.

Visitors often express disappointment at not seeing bears lumber up to the cars in search of handouts. As one told me: "Do you realize I came all the way from New Jersey to see two things — Old Faithful and a real live bear in the open? I mean, look, buddy, seeing a bear running free may not mean much to you, but when you live in Wee-hawken, it can be a big thing in your life."

STILL, THE CARS AND CAMPERS roll into Yellowstone in ever-increasing numbers. I have seen summer traffic on the park's Grand Loop Road backed up bumper-to-bumper. There are traffic signs, and citations for speeding. There are wrecks and wreckers. Campground sites fill up fast, and permits are needed to camp in the back country.

With two million people coming to the park each year in half a million vehicles, Yellowstone, like some other attractions in the Rockies, is troubled by its own popularity. In Montana's Bob Marshall Wilderness, so many people on horseback are moving through that the wildlife has retreated from the vicinity of the trails; grazing by the horses leaves slim pickings for animals native to that spectacular country. At times, it seems as if all the millions of backpackers in this nation, who spent an estimated 300 million dollars in 1975 for equipment alone, have converged on the Rockies.

Crowds or not, there are rewards beyond number:

The bold pink push of flowering moss campion through the soggy snow of early spring on the tundra of Rocky Mountain National Park, and in autumn a family of bighorn sheep with the ram looking down from a ledge like a pasha surveying his harem.

Alpine meadows, and creeks somersaulting with snow melt to feed the two hundred lakes of Glacier National Park, and the bracing breath of ice sheets blowing down snow flurries in July.

Banff and Jasper National Parks in the Canadian Rockies, where the raw strength of the land presses down on the traveler like divine affirmation of the goodness of nature. The high bulk of the mountains prompts a visitor from Colorado to dismiss his native ranges

Lady anglers and their friends — two armed
for grouse hunting — evoke the sport and
scenery of the Montana Rockies in an 1890's pose.

as "anthills," and bighorns linger near the road where tourists toss them chocolate cookies and peanuts and spare apples.

Grand Teton, one of the most popular national parks in the American Rockies, also offers rewards to the visitor, but they are sometimes made flat by the heavy press of commercial development on the rim of the park. The town of Jackson is a carnival of motels and gift shops: "Save your tent — We need the rent" or "a Bronze to hang on your wall . . . just give us a call." Catering to the tourist dollar has prompted affectations of the ways of the Old West, including re-enactment of a shootout in the town square near archways made of elk antlers, no less. Boots beat out a clunking tattoo on wooden side-walks, *new* wooden sidewalks, and dropouts-turned-cowboys cultivate ripening bands of sweat stain on their trail-driver hats.

Inside the park there is a commercial airport, and it has been pro-posed that the facilities be enlarged to accommodate jet aircraft. Not if Margaret Murie can help it.

Mrs. Murie lives within the boundaries of the park, in a hand-some house made of logs. There are others, too, who live in the park,

all on the sites of old homesteads. In some cases, individual ownership has been retained; in many, the property has been acquired by
the government with the provision that the seller may continue
living there under lease arrangements. So it is with Mrs. Murie.

A long-time activist for conservation causes, she recalled the
controversy surrounding enlargement of Grand Teton National
Park in 1943. Her husband, the late Olaus Murie, who at one time was
director of the Wilderness Society, studied the elk of the area for
many years, and he too was a leader of pro-park forces.

"There were a few people in Jackson Hole who realized that this
was an unusual place and should be preserved and not given over to
exploitation or too much private ownership," Mrs. Murie told me.
"This little group went to Mr. John D. Rockefeller, Jr., and asked him
for his help. That was the beginning, in the 1920's. The opposition in
1943 came mostly from cattlemen who felt that the government was
taking too much, encroaching on their individual rights."

Mrs. Murie came to the area in 1927, after graduating from the
University of Alaska (the first woman to do so), and she still looks to
the mountains and the valley with a fresh appreciation every day.

"This house," she said, "was built in 1937 by four Swedish
brothers who were very good logmen. I love living in a log house.
And I'm carrying on what . . . well, I hope I'm doing what Olaus
would have me do by staying here and speaking out for what I think
is right. If I left, I'd be denying everything we lived for."

She went to a window to look for the marten she feeds daily.
"The marten is the most gorgeous mammal in the woods around
here," she said. "We also have eight deer that spend the summer
here, and there're often moose walking through the clearing."

In her 49 years of residence in the valley, she has come to know
wildlife as few persons have. Not far from her home in the park is
the National Elk Refuge, a 23,754-acre haven where as many as 7,500
elk gather in the winter, coming in from higher country. There are
also trumpeter swans on the refuge, along with an assortment of
mule deer, moose, and, of course, coyotes.

As she prepared to go out on her daily jaunt through the cottonwoods and spruce on cross-country skis, Mrs. Murie, who has grandchildren now in college, said she is upset about the undisciplined
surge of growth in Jackson. But she hopes that some of the damage
can be repaired.

Meanwhile, the boom has started to push over the mountains, to
the western side of the Tetons. A resort there, just over the border
from Idaho, offers skiing on a broad, gentle mountain that calls down
incredible amounts of fine snow each year. The valley there lacks the
thumping visual dramatics of the eastern face of the mountains, but
it is one impressive pocket of scenery.

There is a town here called Alta, with an elementary school. Its
enrollment varies—about 30. It may well be the happiest institute of
learning in all the country. It has a single-story building erected
around 1910: two classrooms, a small gym, a library, a lunchroom.

It was the lunchroom, I think, that made me wish I had attended
this school. For the cook is Vada Green and, as most everyone in the

area will tell you, Vada Green is an extraordinary person. She bakes all her bread and cinnamon rolls, she makes the desserts (cakes, or banana sherbet), and she often honors the children's requests in preparing the main course, with pizza a specialty. The students made a poster in her honor: "Vada's Lunches Are Mm-Good."

Mrs. Doris Moss has been teaching there for 18 years, and her former students are forever coming back to see her. Indeed, when the junior high school was closed for a week because of an epidemic of flu, many of the idle students passed the time at Alta elementary.

Children learn quickly and well at this school because the atmosphere is one of great warmth and understanding. For example, Dennis Finch, the other teacher, understands that most of the children have little time for recreation between studying and ranch chores. So he has, on more than one occasion, dismissed school and gone tramping off with the kids to a stream for an afternoon of fishing.

On Fridays, in winter, all of the students go skiing. In late spring, they are taught how to swim. And in the fall, hiking-and-science trips are scheduled—four miles or ten. Mrs. Moss often takes her old horse along, and if one of the students tires from all the walking, she plunks the youngster in the saddle.

For the novice, says a friend of mine, hiking versus horseback is "choosing between blistered feet and bruised rear. A horse gives you a better vantage point in spectacular country like the Wind Rivers, and a packhorse carries fresh meat and produce when a backpacker's down to freeze-dried stuff. But packing and saddling and tending horses takes up time you could spend catching fresh trout—and the horse that carried you 15 miles into the mountains can break loose and trot 15 miles back to the barn out of sheer cussedness."

HIKER AND HORSEMAN will share the border-to-border Continental Divide Trail from Mexico to Canada if and when it reaches completion—possibly about 1995. A draft study has gone back and forth between Denver and Washington, D. C., while officials pondered some interesting questions. Is a trail that the general public can use better than one too difficult for anyone except experts? Are National Forest Service officials right in thinking that any trail would bring too many people into areas designated as wilderness? Given the demands on public moneys, how much should be spent on a trail in the northern regions, where summer would be extremely short in the best of years?

While these debates work themselves out, Canada offers its Great Divide Trail: 350 miles already available, with hundreds of miles in alternative bypaths—more than enough for a full summer's wilderness travel, and access easy enough for a week or weekend.

For some, throughout the Rocky Mountain region, fall is the time for hiking and riding—in search of game. Hunting season.

There are 20 million hunters in this country, and at times it seems as if they are all going for the same animal in the same forest. Years ago, the annual migration of elk from Yellowstone Park coincided with the opening of hunting season in Wyoming. "The hunters would line up, outside the park, and when the elk started to come out, they would be waiting," an observer of the massacre told me. "You didn't need a gun, just a pair of track shoes, because there were so many elk killed that no one knew who shot what. All you had to do was just run to a fallen elk and take it."

The average sportsman in the Mountain West regards his right to hunt as no less sacred than his right to freedom of religion. Of course, there are regulations (in Colorado, for example, the pine squirrel can be taken only between October 1 and January 31), but, still, the urge to shoot sometimes overcomes caution. Deer season had been opened in New Mexico only a few days in 1974 when the death toll reached four—four hunters. One was killed as he carried a slain deer across his back. He was shot by another hunter.

But sooner or later the guns are silent in the Rockies, and then it is time to get back into the forest and wait for one of those magic moments that nature hands out like sweets to a child.

I walked with a friend through shoulder-high clumps of willows bordering the creek, a tributary of the Salmon River in Idaho. Stopping, he pointed at the water—shallow, swift-gaited, full of frothy rips where it broke over rocks. The creek was about 15 feet wide, and near the middle were two large salmon. Suddenly, the female was seized in the furious, flapping delivery of her eggs. The seizures continued on and off until, finally, she lay still again. Wracked by the struggle to reach the spawning grounds, the fish would die soon, most likely within a few days. The waters of the creek would bear the body to rest against a rock, and there this noble death would pass with only the buzzing of flies for a eulogy. Young salmon would inherit the waters in their season, and the wilderness would live by its ancient rhythms under sun and snow.

Slogging uphill through virgin snow, Jack and Ann Uhlenbrock share the exhilaration of backpacking on skis in the isolation of Colorado's White River National Forest. Cross-country touring developed in the 1870's when miners of Scandinavian origin made long wooden skis called "snowshoes" for trips to get supplies—and for their own amusement.

$\mathcal{E}$tching new trails in spring snow, expert skiers swoop down Vowell Glacier in British Columbia's Purcell Mountains—dropping 5,500 feet in elevation. Their luxury

JILL DURRANCE

"lift" flies them back to the top as many times as their endurance holds out. This area, known as the "Bugaboos," offers a hundred high-mountain runs reached only by jet helicopter.

C*risp twilight deepens in Telluride, perched at 8,500 feet in Colorado's San Juan Mountains. In Aspen, in the Sawatch Range, guests linger over dinner on a winter evening. Both towns sprang up as mining camps in the 1870's: Aspen, now a sports and cultural center, wrenched a fortune in silver from nearby lodes; Telluride—prosperous from its gold strikes—built an opera house still used in summer. Today visitors throng to these restored Victorian towns seeking different "treasures" from the Rockies: skiing, hiking, fishing.*

*G*ripping the control
bar of his hang glider
to keep it steady,
Blair Trenholme levels
his "Seagull III" after
takeoff. His landing site:
a narrow beach at the
town of Kaslo, British
Columbia, on Kootenay
Lake—a vertical
drop of 4,500 feet from
the launching point.
A camera rigged on
the back of the glider
let Blair photograph his
own flight as he soared
on thermal air currents.

DICK DURRANCE AND BLAIR TRENHOLME

*W*hen the snows melt, interest in water fun rises with the thermometer. Kayak instructor Kirk Baker—protected from rocks and icy waters by a hockey helmet, rubber drysuit, and life jacket—muscles his way through the white waters of Steel Bridge Rapids near Glenwood Springs, Colorado. Students under Kirk's direction start their lessons on a lake, continue to a "slow-moving river to learn the dynamics of flowing water," and in a week advance to small rapids. Preferring a team effort, rugby aficionados get a vigorous Saturday workout in Aspen's Wagner Park. Aspen's amateurs play teams from all over the western United States and invite them to an increasingly popular "Ruggerfest," a weekend of competition held yearly in late September.

"*Casting the hounds," Colorado huntsman Michael Strang blows the signal on his horn that "sends them all searching their prey's scent." The "field," waiting on a lush meadow before Mount Sopris, will follow the English foxhounds. The Roaring Fork Hounds club obeys the traditional rules of the hunt with one exception: They chase coyotes, not foxes. Some 50 to 60 devotees set out through rough, rocky terrain from "cubbing time in August until the snow's too deep in January." Founded in 1967, the club boasts a perfect record of never catching a coyote. A saddle-bronc rider flies from his seat on a top-of-the-string mount, Two Spot, at an East Helena Valley Rodeo Association competition. Throughout the Rockies, rodeos draw rugged participants and screaming fans.*

JILL DURRANCE (BELOW)

*H*unched under her pack,
*Bettina Watkins crosses Elk Creek
in Colorado with 15 companions
from Telluride Mountaineering
School. Near their destination on
the ten-day trek—Vestal Peak in
the San Juans (opposite)—Sherry
Carlson wears her hard hat for
protection from loose rocks.
Belayed with nylon rope, Laura
Truettner climbs the lichen-
covered face of Vestal. The girls,
age 14 to 19, spend six weeks
learning to live in the wilderness.
After river trips, climbing and
backpacking courses, they make
a six-day desert journey in
southern Utah canyon country.*

Green grass of Wyoming carpets the meadows of the Wind River Range as guide Renny

Debbie Elton (below), a
Colorado native and resi-
dent of Vail, in the Park
Range, found the Wind
Rivers by comparison
"more spectacular and
rugged, with more lakes—
also more mosquitoes."
At dawn, freshly caught
brook trout stir appetites
of the campers.

Burke leads his small camping party along Washakie Creek in the Bridger Wilderness.

A PORTFOLIO OF
A MOUNTAIN TOWN

Kaslo, British Columbia

I WRITE OF A TOWN, a village really, in the shadow of the Rockies. For many months I searched for it, knowing neither its name nor location. In truth, I wasn't searching so much as simply hoping and waiting for the town to reveal itself, to touch me with its peaceableness, to arrest me with its beauty of setting.

Such qualities are common among the towns I visited; but just as there is one agate more perfect than all the others in a bag of marbles, so too is there a town in the Mountain West of singular appeal. This is, of course, a personal judgment.

There is a town in the Canadian province of British Columbia, and its name is Kaslo, and the sight of it will fill you with joy.

You will find it at the juncture of Highways 31 and 31A, up where early darkness races the winter sun. You will find it on a peninsula in a lake that stretches, long and narrow, between two mountain ranges.

I divulge this with reluctance, for Kaslo rests, more or less, in the anonymity of undiscovery. With no public transportation other than the mail bus (six passengers), it takes its visitors in small doses. And that's best, because heavy popularity can sometimes sap the character from a scenic mountain town.

Still, it is possible to get to Kaslo—most easily by car. It's a choice between driving north from Nelson and driving east from New Denver or Galena Bay and then south. Either way, the road is tangled with curves and dark in the shade of heavy forests. The area is known as the Kootenay, and it stretches from the Selkirk and Purcell ranges of the Columbia Mountains eastward into the Rockies. In the middle of it all is Kootenay Lake, measuring about 70 miles from one end to the other and itself a thoroughfare in the heyday of the paddlewheel steamers.

Most of Kaslo sits on the flat, spade-shaped delta that was formed by

Mayor-elect and museum manager for the village of Kaslo, Roy E. Green tends the S. S. Moyie, ashore after 60 years on Kootenay Lake. Last of the sternwheel steamers to ply these waters, she became a museum in 1958.

a river-borne wash of gravel to the lake. The upper end of the town pushes against the foothills of mountains. Across the lake, less than a mile away, more mountains rise behind the timbered hills that reach down to the strip of sandy beach.

It is scenery that falls on the viewer like a blanket, snuffing out all the little fires of human hatred.

I parked my car and walked the length of Front Street, past Jiggs' Place and Kaslo Shoe Repair and the Bank of Montreal; past the government liquor store and the community bulletin board with its posted offerings of goats for sale; past the S. S. *Moyie* where Roy Green was standing on deck like a master staring down the wrath of a gale at sea.

The S. S. *Moyie* is a sternwheel steamer that once plied the lake. Stranded permanently on blocks at the foot of Front Street, it is now a museum which Roy Green tends. He was never a seaman, but there is a light seasoning of the nautical in his vocabulary. I asked him about the town, and he sat me down to listen.

"Back at the turn of the century there were 3,000 to 5,000 people in Kaslo," he said. "It was a floating population. Mining brought the men in and out. Now there's about 800 of us living here. We're a growing population of retired people—old-age pensioners. Public works take care of a few, and a little bit of tourist trade and the services that go along with that. Mostly, we depend on logging operations and small sawmill operations. But, you know, making a living is just something we refuse to worry about because it just seems to come naturally."

Roy Green is 76 years old. He has lived in Kaslo most of his life. "I've sat down and asked myself what am I doing stuck away back here in this isolated part of the world when things are happening outside," he said. "But after a little further reflection I say, well, where could I do better?"

So he's there most every day, aboard the paddlewheeler, greeting those who stop by to see the exhibits. In midmorning, his dog at his heels, he strolls down the street for coffee and conversation with longtime friends. And they remember:

Floods and fires that in years past reduced whole blocks to rubble.

Miners at work, "rawhiding" the ore down the mountains with the use of horses outfitted in wooden snowshoes.

The saloons, and the Chinese wash houses, and the painted ladies (permitted to shop on Front Street, but only on Thursdays).

Members of the Band of Hope, a temperance organization, marching along Front Street in the 1920's, chanting, ". . . the Drink, it paints men's noses red, and blights their lives, and kills them dead—We'll fight until it's van-quish-ed. Hurrah! Hurrah! Hurrah!"

Once, Kaslo had 14 barbers and one schoolteacher. It now has two part-time barbers and 16 schoolteachers. It follows, then, that there are long-haired students at work in the sunny classrooms of the one schoolhouse in town. "We really don't give much concern to how they wear their hair or how they dress," Jack Humphries, school principal, told me. "I just tell them not to wear these things as a badge. Really, these are the best kids—they're fine."

I joined him and his wife for lunch in their 75-year-old house, a rambling three-story structure on a shaded corner lot. The yard was full of lilacs and rhododendrons, and rich fragrances were stirred and carried on a breeze that pushed through the open windows. "We've had bears come right into the yard," Humphries said. "When there are not many berries in the woods, they come into town to raid the orchards."

There are both grizzlies and black bear in the area. White-tailed deer come down in winter and walk the beaches. Ospreys circle over the lake, diving on fish in ballets of swift, sure movements.

It was early morning and there was a play of coppery light on Mount Loki, the highest mountain in view from the town. Bruce Tate and I were out on the lake, and he pointed to a cabin partially hidden in the trees. "An old prospector has lived there for years," he told me. "Now and then he comes to Kaslo for supplies."

There are others living in those seemingly impenetrable mountains, I learned; not many, but some. They are men who have escaped unto themselves, seeing no one, alone and liking it. They trap, and search for valuable minerals. Occasionally they come to Kaslo for tobacco and a meal in a restaurant. They don't stay long.

We threaded the narrow lake for 20 or 30 miles in Tate's small motor-boat as he pointed out familiar canyons and bays. In his 20 years of residence in Kaslo, where he now owns a motel, he has come to know the lake well. He never tires of its splendor.

IN 1890 it held no less appeal for George Thomas Kane, who got the town started. His brother, David, had a bear for a pet, but it had to be destroyed because it developed a fondness for eating small dogs. Miners and loggers followed Kane to the region, and before the century had turned, Kaslo was caught up in a storm of activity. Miss McLeod opened her clothing store, offering "a stock of Millinery, Ladies' suits and Fancy Goods, Second to none in the Kootenays." Otto Augustine ("a stalwart representative of Sweden") presided over the Silver King Hotel, while James W. Cockle found a 120-ton boulder of solid galena ore back in the hills.

The Kaslo Board of Trade boasted in 1899 that only 31 deaths had occurred in the first eight years of the town's existence. And hear why: "... cleanliness and strict attention to every necessity conducive to health is scrupulously observed by those in authority."

Well, yes, Kaslo is clean. It's frayed, but clean. City Hall is almost 80 years old, but it's a good building, a monument to the enduring dignity of wood. Once there was talk of replacing it, but that's stopped now; preservation has become a worthy cause.

There isn't much to preserve. The old opera house was torn down long ago. The town is without a trolley barn, or even a replica of Irish castle erected by some eccentric mining magnate. None of that.

Kaslo's history lacks dazzle. Economically, the town's best days were during its infancy. As yet it has given the world neither a major poet nor a Wimbledon champion. It is a place of gentle simplicity, where a girl named Margaret is born and raised, and, upon her graduation from high school, reads in the yearbook: "Marg's greatest ambition is to become a hairdresser and play a fiddle—and we don't mean second. Her pet peeve is Leona. Marg will probably be moving to Trail."

That's what many do—graduate and move to Trail, or to Nelson, or Vancouver. But the exodus of the young has started to slacken. "The trend is changing now," Roy Green said. "The young people are beginning to take an interest in their own locality; they're beginning to understand how beautiful it is here. There is a very close contact with nature to be had in this area, and that can occupy a young person more than a street corner or a drugstore or a poolroom."

Young people from other places are coming to Kaslo. That has caused concern among long-time residents, for some of the newcomers are without funds. Hippie is a word heard often these days in Kaslo.

"I call them bush tourists, because that's where they live, in the bush." The old logger raised his glass and the beer splashed against his mustache. "But, hell, they're good kids. They've got a better appreciation for the land than most of us old coots."

Over the years, Kaslo has drawn settlers from distant shores—Finns and Dutch and Swedes. Japanese-Canadians were sent there during World War II for detention, and when the fighting stopped, there were those who elected to stay. A fair number of the young people who are finding their way there these days are from the United States.

One day in late May of each year is set aside for a celebration in Kaslo. It honors the late Queen Victoria, who was born on May 24. There is a parade, with sports events, and hearty consumption of beer. It's been going on for 84 years, but it's different now. They no longer have rock-drilling and bannock-baking contests or mule races on Front Street with the riders facing tailward.

"That's all gone now," Roy Green said with a trace of regret. "All gone. Now the activities are concentrated in the park. But it's a pretty park, isn't it?" It's down by the lake, and in the late afternoons of summer, the light there is shafted through the cottonwoods to fall in leafy patterns on the grass.

Yes, it's a pretty park.

Quiet autumn amble belies Front Street's stormy past. Kaslo's main street has survived devastating fires, floods, and the roaring days of the mining boom.

*S*ummer-morning mist thins out to unveil Kaslo, sheltered by forest on Kootenay Lake's western shore in Canada's Mountain West. After decades of population decline, the

community now attracts settlers young and old, and an increasing number of visitors come to share its outdoor diversions—boating, fishing, hiking, deer and bear hunting.

Wood and woodworking sustain Kaslo. Ex-lumberman "Happy" Cappy Jacura (below) crafts rare burls into furniture. A 25-year resident, he declares that newcomers make "the rest of us stop long enough to take a look at the overpowering beauty around here." Tomio Baba, master boatbuilder (left), mends a loggers' boat. Relocated during World War II with hundreds of other coastal Japanese-Canadians, he stayed; he now works in a sawmill. As in many mountain villages, job scarcity plagues Kaslo. Greg Fedoruk lost his job switching lumber-laden boxcars after rail-barge service stopped, and has left to seek work "up north." But many unemployed stay on in Kaslo, with short-term jobs and government assistance.

*R*etired but involved, Mayor Ardus
Colter won his term of office after just four
years in Kaslo. A pensioner, like many of
the townspeople, he says: "If you don't
like the rat race, it's a nice place to live."

*"O*ld-timers and newcomers, they're good people in this town," says Father
Joseph Anthony Boyle. He has just celebrated Mass for his parishioners
at Sacred Heart Roman Catholic Church, where he has served since 1940.

*P*aul *Bunyans with bulldozers, Bill Seafoot (above) and his crew of 19 harvest spruce and balsam near Mount Cooper, about 30 miles north of Kaslo. After the "faller" has cut down the tree and "bucked" or sawed it into 35- to 40-foot logs, "chokerman" Bill Gordon (left) sets the choker cable around the log. A Caterpillar will then haul it to the logging truck, to reach the mill by road and water. Timber has replaced Kaslo's turn-of-the-century mainstay, the silver, zinc, and lead ore that drew an all-time-high population of 5,000. Logging, under license in Crown forests, provides the major source of income now, employing more than 100 of today's 800 residents at least part of the year. And it means big money for some: A skilled faller might earn more than $120 a day, 10 or 11 months of the year; a chokerman, $65.*

*K*aslo's young arrivals bring new ideas and recycle the old. A sunny Sunday morning draws volunteers (right) for work restoring the 82-year-old Langham, once an elegant rooming house. In 1974 a group of newcomers formed the Langham Cultural Society to preserve the structure and to furnish facilities for the arts. Now a $28,000 government grant speeds the project, providing seven paid jobs. Jim Van Horn (below), a plumber and a founder of the society, splits logs near the house he built with his wife, Fern. Chosen alderman after only two years in Kaslo, Jim came to the village seeking beauty and a "more relaxed" existence, where the "land does not get ripped off." Despite some resistance from old-timers, he sees his chosen home as a "rather unique town, a mixed group of people . . . now being accepted." Many of his contemporaries agree. Artist Minto Purvitis (left), one of those attracted here, sketches at the Kaslo Hotel. Jim Van Horn sums it up: "Kaslo is almost Paradise for a lot of people."

CHAPTER FOUR

Those Who Suffered the Most...

SUNLIGHT GLINTED off the hulk of the '53 Chevy that lay in the ditch where a diseased dog licked the inside of an empty tuna-fish can. Two children, each with moisture trailing from the nose, sat nearby in rank weeds, hurling stones across the road. Angry, drunken voices spilled from a house through a door of torn, greasy screen—a late-night argument at two o'clock in the afternoon. This was Browning, Montana, on the reservation of the Blackfeet Indians.

Earl Old Person, tribal council chairman, traced a pattern in the sweat on a can of Coke and said: "The Bureau of Indian Affairs claims the unemployment rate on the reservation is 28 percent, but it's about 60 percent. We know that to be a fact. It seems that we fail to speak the same language as the BIA much of the time."

There are indeed many hardships on this reservation abutting Glacier National Park. Employment is uncertain. Inactivity is stifling. Despair is widespread. Some of the young are filled with an anger that strains against the confines of nonviolence.

"Our young people want things done now," Old Person said. "When we're told by the BIA to do something, we rush to do it. And then they keep us waiting." Clearly, the Bureau of Indian Affairs is out of favor with the Blackfeet of Montana, as it is with most of the other 131,694 Indians on reservations in the Mountain West. It is aged animosity, but the rumblings grow louder.

The Blackfeet Reservation sprawls over nearly a million acres. Living on and adjacent to the reservation are 6,200 Blackfeet, with total tribal enrollment about double that. They are among the minorities—blacks, Mexican-Americans, Mormons—whose roots are entwined in the early history of the Mountain West, and whose presence today is bringing about changes in the social structure.

Indian-turned-cowboy, Ray Mirabol tends his son's cattle on snow-dappled tribal land near Taos Pueblo, New Mexico. Preserving ancient customs of a farming tradition, some Taos Indians have become ranchers.

The lieutenant-governor of Colorado is black, and the governor of New Mexico a Hispano. Bilingual education is mandatory in some Denver schools, and women are now eligible for admission to the Air Force Academy at Colorado Springs. It is the Indian, however, whose strides for change are stirring the most dust.

The tears over broken treaties are gone, dried by the fires of a new militancy. "I don't even want to talk to you about our problems because you can't understand," an Indian of about 25 years said to me as he sat in the BIA office in Browning, a sheaf of government forms in his hand. "I will tell you this, though: We're going to get what belongs to us, and if that means taking it, it will be taken."

Even as he spoke, Blackfeet officials were petitioning the Secretary of the Interior to recognize rights secured by a document signed in 1895 — including rights to water. At that time, they claimed, it was agreed that members of the tribe would have free access to, and the right to hunt and fish and take timber on, lands that were brought within the boundaries of Glacier National Park 15 years later.

In years long past, a show of anger by the Blackfeet would have struck fear into many. White trappers knew the Blackfeet as easily provoked to do battle. Other tribes tended to avoid encounters with the Blackfeet, for they too recognized them as superior warriors. Thus Blackfeet country was among the last to be settled.

AS MEMBERS of a three-tribe confederation — the other two being Piegan and Blood — the Blackfeet controlled territory that stretched from the North Saskatchewan River in Canada to the southern headstreams of the Missouri River in Montana. Pressure on the tribe intensified with the push West by land-seekers and prospectors (there is irony in Indians' having been expelled from their land because of the white man's greed for gold, only to be resettled on lands laden with the new treasure of our time — coal). They struck out against the intruders, attacking ranches and even forts. Retaliation was severe, however, and the Blackfeet began to know defeat.

At the same time, the buffalo was disappearing, and there was hunger in the tribe. Disease claimed many lives. Finally, by 1888, all of the Blackfeet in this country were relocated on the reservation.

The government tried to make farmers of the Blackfeet, but there was resistance. The white man's work ethic was alien to the Indian for many reasons, and none of them had to do with laziness. For some Indians, earth was mother, and to farm was to tear her flesh. A Nez Perce named Smohalla, more than 100 years ago, could say this:

"My young men shall never work. Men who work cannot dream; and wisdom comes to us in dreams. You ask me to plow the ground. Shall I take a knife and tear my mother's breast? Then when I die she will not take me to her bosom to rest. You ask me to dig for stone. Shall I dig under her skin for her bones? Then when I die I cannot enter her body to be born again. You ask me to cut grass and make hay and sell it and be rich like white men. But how dare I cut off my mother's hair?"

Still, the Blackfeet eventually turned to the land, and today some of them derive an income from agriculture and cattle operations. Most, however, are without employment.

"The lack of work is our biggest problem," Earl Old Person said. "The tribal council has done everything to try to create jobs. We were fortunate enough to work out a small sawmill operation on the reservation, and that employed about 45 people. We were expanding and doing well, but this spring there was a fire and the mill was badly damaged. In 1972 we started our Blackfeet Indian Writing Company, and now there are close to 70 people working there. We make ballpoints, felt-tips—a complete line."

The average per capita income on the reservation is $1,500 a year. "The federal government is building homes for the Blackfeet," Old Person said, "but the people with the most critical need are not getting in them because of age or income rules and requirements."

James Welch, a Blackfeet Indian, has made a strong statement about the desperation of life on the reservation. His novel *Winter In the Blood*, published in 1974, is free of protest and rich in beauty, but each of the 176 pages touches on the black emptiness of a life—an Indian's life—that unconsciously dulls pain with indifference. Welch's Indian can attend a funeral and watch as the coffin bearing the body of an old Indian woman is lowered into the grave. But the hole is not large enough, and one end of the coffin rests against the dirt wall. There is concern that the head of the corpse is in the lower end.

The scene is an invitation to rage—to scream at a denial of dignity even in death. But Welch has his man observing passively as "Lame Bull lowered himself into the grave and jumped up and down on the high end." Yet this scene ends with dignity. Only an Indian could write with truth in crafting such a complex reaction, for, as Welch points out in a note on the dustjacket of the book, "Whites have to adopt a stance; Indians already have one."

Jim Welch is a soft-spoken, humorous man of 35. He is a published poet as well as a novelist, and when he talks about his boyhood on reservations, his words are lifted from wells of gentle emotion.

As a youngster on the reservation at Browning, he lived with his parents and two brothers in two small rooms. "I wasn't aware then that the reservation was a dismal place," he told me. "It seemed ideal; we could hunt muskrats in the potholes, and we could go next door to Glacier National Park to picnic."

The family moved to the Fort Belknap Reservation in north-central Montana while Jim was still attending elementary school. Then, in the nearby town of Harlem, he encountered the painful reality of discrimination. "There were signs in the windows of some of the bars in Harlem that read 'Dogs and Indians not allowed,'" he said. The next move was to Minneapolis, where he graduated from high school. He obtained a degree from Northern Montana College; after that he came to Missoula, where he has lived ever since.

"Social concern didn't exist on the reservations when I was there," he said. "Our concern was for economic survival. We had meat on the table because my dad hunted a lot, including poaching in the park. He would go there and take an elk, as did many others on the reservation. It was a way of life."

Guardian of a sacred
The Blackfeet Indians,

EDWARD S. CURTIS

Now, Jim returns occasionally to the reservation at Browning, and always with a feeling, he said, of strong attachment: "My roots are there. I feel close to the people, the land, the mountains, the whole works. When I'm back there, I'm comfortable."

Jim Welch walks the dusty roads on the reservation and remembers: tales of great buffalo hunts passed on by his father, who heard them from his grandmother; the oil companies that came onto the reservation in the 1950's, drilled their wells, capped them, and then went away; his friend from school days, a sensitive, brilliant Blackfeet who, unable to cope with the pressures of the outside world, drank himself to death before the age of 30.

He will call on his memories for the books he hopes to write. Meanwhile, his concern for the welfare of his people grows deeper.

And there is a white man whose concern rises above the widespread indifference among those on the outside. His name is Mel Ruder, and he publishes and edits the weekly *Hungry Horse News* in Columbia Falls, Montana. After teaching journalism and serving in the Navy, in 1946 he started the paper in the small town on the western rim of Glacier National Park.

Mel Ruder's love is photography, and from the start he has filled the *News* with good pictures. In early June of 1964, when the area was getting the melt of heavy snows of the previous winter, it started to rain — and it rained until the accumulation reached 16 inches. There was a flood. Thirty people were killed. Ruder was on the scene to record the tragedy with his camera and notebook. For this work, he was awarded the 1965 Pulitzer Prize for general reporting.

"I came here because I wanted to live near the mountains and take pictures," he said. "In '37 I spent a week with William Henry Jackson, the great photographer of the West who was then about 94; and I worked under Jack Haines, 'Mr. Yellowstone,' for two summers."

He is a man of compassion and boundless energy who suggests to his wife that she put her hands over her ears when he is about to utter a mild curse word. He often visits the Blackfeet Reservation where, he said, he has observed signs of a growing militancy. "It's disturbing," he told me. "There's only one real answer to the problems of the Blackfeet, and that's education and acquiring job skills."

"The teaching staff at Heart Butte started Tuesday morning enrolling children. There are five teachers. The children should learn something."

That news item appeared in the *Glacier Reporter*, a weekly newspaper published in Browning. The author was John Tatsey, whose Indian name was Weasel Necklace. He was a long-time tribal policeman on the reservation, and a correspondent whose reports to the paper have been inserted in the *Congressional Record*. Little that

Blackfeet medicine pipe in the early 1900's, Bear Bull wears the coiled braid of his office.
renowned as warriors and hunters, once roamed the Western plains following bison herds.

happened on the reservation ever escaped his attention. For example:

"Mr. Richard Little Dog has been coming to Heart Butte on Sundays. Tatsey had to put him in jail for the night. He came again last Sunday and someone reported so the police went to investigate, found him out in a car. Police asked his wife what was wrong. She said he was sick and his heart was stopping on him coming from Browning and stopped altogether when they got to Heart Butte. Police told them to leave and Richard's heart got back in motion. Too much Gallo."

Too much Gallo. The phrase appeared frequently in Tatsey's reports, underscoring a problem of some dimension. Men like Mel Ruder hope that education will help cork the wine bottle.

A unique school in the Mountain West is the Institute of American Indian Arts, in Santa Fe, New Mexico. Founded in 1962, it provides education for Indians, Eskimos, and Aleuts with talents in the fine arts. Enrollment stood at 150 in 1975.

"We would like to increase that to 250," Chuck Poitras, associate director, said. "We have over 100 acres of grounds here, so there is lots of room for expansion. But the Bureau of Indian Affairs, the institute's parent organization, has not yet recognized the significance of this type of education."

It was November when I visited the institute, and the campus was freighted with leaves from the many cottonwoods. The grounds ran flat, seemingly to the distant Sangre de Cristo Mountains flushed at this sunset with fading light. Since then, the BIA has chartered the school as a junior college and Chuck Poitras reports plans for a new outreach program for Indian communities.

Most of the emphasis at the institute is on painting, sculpture, and creative writing. All have taken new directions in recent years. No longer do the paintings take the form of traditional Indian art — the two-dimensional, decorative, highly stylized designs found on baskets and pottery. Now, much of the art reflects the protest that brought about Wounded Knee II, and the occupation of Alcatraz.

Yes, there are still depictions of braves astride ponies, bare-chested, arrow-armed, face to the wind. But there are more with the imagery of anger and the unforgiveness of past injustices.

And there are some in which the strength of protest spirit is invested with a gentleness, such as a poem called "Laughing Bowl" by Donna Whitewing, a Winnebago-Sioux:

> I cried because I didn't have
> A little bitty slice of something else;
> Then the sun reached down
>   and tickled my tears
> I made a laughing bowl
>   that caught the tears
> To wash the hand that touched me.

With its location in Santa Fe, the institute is in an area of the Rockies where the influence of the minorities carries more flavors than one — not only of the sun symbol sacred to the Indians of the Southwest, but also of the sword and banners of Old Spain, the past of the conquistadors. For it was here, in this city which had a governor's palace before the coming of the Pilgrims, that the Spanish stamped this land with a culture that has endured until this day.

They arrived in the 1530's, the first non-Indians to reach the Rockies. Movement to the mountains was from the south then — from Mexico — and the explorers were seeking the fabled Seven Cities of Cibola, each believed to hold great wealth. Among those hunting treasure was Francisco Vásquez de Coronado, and from 1540 to 1542 he moved through New Mexico and Arizona. He found only the pueblos of Indians. The new land was desolate and useless, he reported, and forty years passed before another expedition set out. This time the object was slave labor — Indians — for silver mines in the south.

By 1598, a Spanish colony had been established at the pueblo of San Juan de Los Caballeros, near the Chama River. Its founder was Juan de Oñate, who became governor of the province of Nueva Mexico. In 1610 the provincial capital was moved to Santa Fe, making that city the oldest seat of government in the United States.

FROM THE START, many Spanish officials treated the Indians like savages, setting them to forced labor. Meanwhile, missionaries of the Roman Catholic Church were working to convert the natives to Christianity. Missions were built, and the friars touched many with the ritual of baptism. The time came, though, when Indians began to revolt, to wash their bodies as a means of erasing the baptism, and to take up arms against the Spanish. Finally the province settled down to a spotty peace, with intermittent war between the Indian and the white man who came riding the animal with big teeth.

War on a larger scale ended in 1848 with the treaty of Guadalupe Hidalgo and Mexico's cession of her northern lands to the United States. Residents (and later immigrants) would become Mexican-Americans. They would also become the second largest minority in the country, and the last to form a protest movement for their rights.

Today there are perhaps six million Mexican-Americans in the United States. Until the mid-1960's they bore a dual oppression of poverty and contempt — and they bore it in a land discovered and settled by their forefathers. One sympathetic journalist noted in 1941: "they make few complaints . . . which usually go unheard."

But in 1965 Cesar Chavez stirred nationwide interest in the cause of the migrant farm workers in California, the stooped laborers who spoke Spanish and could not vote because of literacy requirements — literacy in English. Striking grape workers declared: "we are pioneers who blaze a trail out of the wilderness of hunger and deprivation that we have suffered even as our ancestors did." Chicano, once a label of condescension, became for many a badge of pride.

In Denver, a militant Chicano named Rodolfo "Corky" Gonzales formed *La Crusada Para la Justicia*, Crusade for Justice. One of its agencies is Escuela Tlatelolco, a school financed by private funds. There, for example, fourth-graders learn to produce a newspaper, because the press is an important agent of political change. A poster in their classroom asserts: "No man has the right to oppress people and all oppressed people have the right to revolution."

And so a long silence has been broken. There are voices — loud, angry voices — calling attention to the old Spanish and Mexican land grants. The treaty of 1848 guaranteed "property of every kind." But the bounds of the grants were not always certain; many of the records were lost; and the amounts of land were vast, and valuable.

For example, near the city of Chama in New Mexico, a roadside marker identifies the area as a land grant of 600,000 acres made to one José Manuel Martinez in 1832. Many of his descendants continue to live there. More legendary is the million-acre Sangre de Cristo grant in Colorado's San Luis Valley. There have been troubles over that land, as with other tracts in the Mountain West.

An Easterner bought the last unfenced section, 77,000 acres, in 1960. He closed the roads, fenced the land, and denied access. The valley people, mostly Hispano, were outraged, claiming they held inherited rights to use of the land — grazing, hunting, fishing, gathering piñon branches for stovewood — from the original grantee. A range war flared for a year and a half until the governor of Colorado intervened. In 1974 there were more troubles, with reports of vandalism and violence. The disputes centered on the rights of the minority (not exactly the minority, for of the 3,000 people in Costilla County, the 1970 census listed 2,400 as of Spanish origin).

More than 80 years have passed since Frederick Jackson Turner proclaimed that "the most important effect of the frontier has been in the promotion of democracy." His words epitomize the great American myth about the West. But Professor Turner, influential historian though he was, had overlooked something.

Bigotry in frontier life ran deep. It promoted democracy, but democracy for whites only. In his book *The Black West: A Documentary and Pictorial History*, William Loren Katz lays the myth bare:

"It has been one of our enduring myths that the western lands offered people — all people — an escape from the inhibiting social customs and mores of the East, that the frontier environment was a stage upon which each performer would be judged by his performance, not his ancestry, sex, color, or wealth. . . . But the black person who came west, whether slave, slave runaway or free man, found neither social mobility, social acceptance, nor an absence of inhibiting customs and laws. He often found that he could not even enter a western territory or state because their earliest laws prohibited the migration of black people. . . . Even the westerner's vaunted antislavery posture stemmed from his colorphobia."

There was Horace Greeley, preaching "go West, young man." And there was Horace Greeley, urging that the frontier "be reserved for the benefit of the white Caucasian race."

But the blacks came. They came as cowboys and soldiers, trappers and homesteaders. There were black cattle rustlers and black rodeo performers. Following the Civil War, blacks came in large numbers as members of the cavalry. Having secured their freedom by then, they came as soldiers to help strip the Indian of his freedom. "The black regiments on the frontier carried forth the genocidal policies of their white officers and government," writes Katz.

Today, the largest black population of the Mountain West is in

Denver. This is mostly a middle-class concentration, with the level of education averaging out at the 12th grade. It is in Colorado, too, that a black has reached high political office.

George Brown is lieutenant-governor of the state. On a day in June of 1975, Brown was involved in a situation that spotlighted the growing influence of minorities in the Rockies. Richard Lamm, the governor, had to travel outside of the state, leaving Brown as the chief executive officer. Brown, in turn, had to leave, and that put Ruben Valdez, speaker of the House of Representatives, in charge. It was the first time in Colorado's history—and possibly the history of the country—that an Anglo, a black, and a Hispano all served as governor of the same state on the same day.

Had one of the three office-holders been a Mormon, the exercise of political roulette would have embraced the minority most responsible for shaping social structures in the Mountain West.

There are more than one million Mormons, or members of the Church of Jesus Christ of Latter-day Saints, in the six-state region, with the largest number—about 830,000—living in Utah. It was in Salt Lake City that they built their greatest temple—in the area Brigham Young called "Deseret." They first arrived in the 1840's, followers of Joseph Smith in search of a haven from persecution, and until this day their numbers and influence have continued to grow.

The church, with a world membership now of 3.4 million, is a force with an impact that reaches beyond the spiritual. For example, it has its own welfare program, a service which distributed more

Horse-drawn travois carries the possessions of a Blackfeet couple across a shrunken domain. In 1888 the federal government restricted the tribe to a 942,045-acre reservation east of the Montana Rockies.

EDWARD S. CURTIS

than 20 million dollars in the calendar year 1974. This is financed by the tithes, contributions, and business income that flow in to the church at an estimated rate of three million dollars a day.

The influence of the church is felt not only in Salt Lake City, but also in many of the small mountain towns that started as settlements designed to offer protection and isolation for those who believed that Joseph Smith received his revelations from the Lord.

The Bear Lake region is such a place.

Reaching across the border of Utah and Idaho, Bear Lake rests like a mitre for one of nature's bishops in the Rockies. This valley is spotted with small towns, the largest being Montpelier, in Idaho. There are Paris and Bloomington and St. Charles, Fish Haven, Dingle and Garden City. And Ovid and Liberty, and, out a way, Georgetown. Until recent years the crush of tourism had spared the valley; but now Bear Lake is stirred to froth by the props of sporty outboards and its blessed isolation is coming to an end.

BEAR LAKE VALLEY was settled in 1863. At that time, the land was under the stewardship of the Shoshone and the Bannock Indians. The Shoshone chief Washakie was a friend of Brigham Young and he agreed to open the valley to the Mormons. They came by the hundred, establishing their settlements with the houses in a cluster because they were one and the land was for all—land that swelled as it ran to the calm waters of the lake, carrying heavy growths of juniper pine, balsam, and quaking aspen.

Before long, Francis M. Pomeroy had built the first flour mill in the valley, and Nathan Davis's sawmill was in operation. William Hulme planted the first apple trees, having traveled by snowshoe to pack the saplings over the mountains.

Peace had come to these Mormons. Nonmembers of the church, "Gentiles" as they were called, were few in number. "We had only one infallible sure rule to telling a Gentile from a Mormon," Joseph C. Rich, son of the Mormon apostle Charles C. Rich who founded the Bear Lake settlement, recalled in his late years. "In those days the people made their own soap and it was accepted as a demonstrated fact that Mormon home-made soap would not lather on a Gentile until he had been in the valley at least a year."

Mormon seclusion in the lovely valley was shattered with the arrival of the railroad in 1880. Montpelier was split along religious lines: Mormons uptown and Gentiles downtown. A fence ran north and south along 8th Street, and that was the dividing line.

Before long, Mormons were reciting their version of the poem called "The Iron Horse." Among the localized verses was this:

> We've been isolated till this day
> hoping somehow that way to stay.
> Now, through our lovely mountain region
> folks will learn of our religion.
> They'll complain about our wives,
> claim we hold them in our hives,
> but it's the railroad that will bring the dives
> which will ruin and cost us happy lives.

"The railroad brought many changes," J. Pat Wilde, Montpelier High School librarian and local historian, told me. "For example, better schools opened—the Mormons just didn't have enough qualified teachers. One of the new schools was established by Presbyterians, and it would have 'spell down' and 'read down' competitions with the Mormon school. Only two records of the competition still exist, and both show the Presbyterians as winners."

Montpelier today is a peaceable town. At night, the large "M" on the hill overlooking the town—an inspiration of the high school graduating class of 1927—lights up. On Washington Street, the E. L. Burgoyne & Sons clothing store continues to do business as it has for a century or more, and the drugstore carries a full line of books on the teachings of the Latter-day Saints. The 8th Street fence is down, and there are Presbyterians uptown.

In the small towns bordering the 19-mile-long lake—Paris, for example, with its Mormon tabernacle large enough to serve a community ten times the size—there are still some strains of resentment against the breaching of the isolation. In the cafes, when the men get a snack, the talk is often of the foibles of newcomers.

But in Garden City, on the Utah end of the lake, one of the few non-Mormons in town was elected mayor. Fred Selle said he moved from Salt Lake City to find a more relaxed way of life. "I think," he said, "there are two other families in town who are not Mormon. There may even be one more than that, but I can't think right offhand who it is." He and his wife, who is the town clerk, operate a general store.

There is another mayor in the Mountain West whose election signals change. This mayor is a woman—a black woman. Her name is Ada Evans, and she and her family are the only blacks in Fairplay, Colorado, a town of 500 people cradled among some of the highest peaks in the Rockies. Her elected position carries no salary, but that makes her no less determined to get the streets paved.

It was in the territories of the Mountain West that women were first granted suffrage. In 1890 Wyoming became the first state to provide for this equality in its constitution. The next three states to adopt female suffrage were Colorado, Utah, and Idaho. Not until 1910 did a state outside of the Rockies grant this right to women.

The early history of the region can hardly exclude its "Ladies of the Lamplight," as they have been called. There were "Poker Alice," a cigar-smoking marvel at stud poker, and Mollie May, whose houses of pleasure in Leadville were among the most famous of the gold-rush era. When she died, the local newspaper printed a poem in her memory, with the lines: "Keep her impurity/In dark obscurity. . . ."

But if there was a Mollie May, there was also a Helen Hunt Jackson, wife of a Colorado Springs banker, a woman who tried as hard as anyone to improve living conditions for the Indians. As a prolific writer, Mrs. Jackson trained her words of protest on the plight of Indians. One of her most famous works was *A Century of Dishonor*, published in 1881. It was a sweeping documentation of how Indian affairs were being mismanaged by the federal government.

Were she alive today, Helen Hunt Jackson would probably have something to say about the eagle feather situation. Such feathers are important elements in many ceremonial and religious activities, but Indians have often been arrested for having the feathers in their possession. It wasn't until early in 1975 that Rogers C. B. Morton, Secretary of the Interior, ruled that Indians may possess and exchange eagle feathers without being in violation of federal laws.

Thus has come into being one of the unique federal agency operations in the history of this country. In Pocatello, Idaho, the U. S. Fish and Wildlife Service has a stock of feathers for use by Indians in religious and ceremonial affairs. At last count, the agency had about 190 golden eagle carcasses on hand, feathers and all.

Morton's action was prompted in part by protest. So it is with most gains made by Indians in the Mountain West today. One tribe even declared "war" on the United States to obtain its demands. But it was a nice war, and the tribe profited beyond its expectations.

There are fewer than 75 members of the Kootenai tribe at Bonners Ferry, Idaho. In 1974, they decided they had been pushed around enough. Their ancestral land was gone, signed away in 1855 without their approval. Conditions on the small reservation were deteriorating.

The Kootenais went on the warpath. First off, they established toll points on both sides of Bonners Ferry. Motorists were asked to pay a dime to drive over the ancestral land. State troopers were ordered to the scene, but there were no arrests. Amy Trice, tribal chairwoman, recalls that the troopers came with shotguns, while they, the Indians, had nothing but a flyswatter in the tribal office.

At the end of four days, $1,500 in dimes had been collected. There was talk of more roadblocks and other maneuvers. Then, the government began to respond; more than that, the response nearly overwhelmed the Indians. They got a road to the reservation, a new housing program, a new water and sewage system, and more. In all, the assistance amounted to almost half a million dollars.

But along with it came the usual blitzkrieg of government forms. Amy Trice calls that "white tape."

Camped on summer pasture near Telluride, Basque sheepherder Francisco Picabea relaxes with his dog after a long day. He works the herder's seven-day week 50 weeks of the year, taking his flock to Utah in winter. Long in demand by American sheep ranchers, Basques have come from Spain by special permit; "Frank" arrived in the Rockies 16 years ago.

Spring roundup in the San Miguel foothills brings Basque sheepherders Jesus Barayazarra (left) and José María García back to the home corrals. Ranch owner Albert Aldasoro

whose daughters welcome the flock, now owns an 8,000-acre spread. His father,
a Basque who had herded sheep in Utah, began buying land in Colorado in 1925.

*I*n the tradition of his forefathers, Spanish-American miller Laurino Cordova and his wife grow wheat and corn on a small farm near Vadito, New Mexico. He traces his ancestry to conquistadors who settled in the Rockies during the 16th century. Below, he fills a sack with stone-ground flour; classes of schoolchildren often visit the water-powered mill to hear Laurino explain the process. The Cordovas' children have chosen city careers; the parents live much as Spanish country people used to do. Beaming, Laurino emerges from the chicken coop with fresh eggs for the kitchen.

*I*n the heart of Ranchos de Taos, New Mexico, stands an adobe
church, recently restored to commemorate the town's Spanish
colonial heritage. Founded in the early 18th century as a Roman
Catholic mission, the Church of St. Francis of Assisi retains many
of its original paintings, altar screens, pieces of silverwork, and
Santos—wooden statues carved by the Spanish settlers. To the
south, the older town of Chimayo has kept its famed Santuario
since 1816; the original crucifix still hangs above the altar, where
feather flowers from Mexico attest the devotion of pilgrims. An
unknown folk artist carved limbs, head, and torso out of soft,
dried cottonwood root. He pegged the sections together, covered
the figure with gesso, and painted on the clear, vibrant colors.

*S*houting over the clatter of a potato harvester, Chicano farm workers *near* Center, Colorado, try to carry on a conversation. Most Chicanos first came to the Rockies from Mexico to find jobs as migratory laborers. Today, *growing* Chicano populations in Western cities strive to improve their standard of living. At La Clinica de la Gente in Santa Fe (below, left), Dr. Bob Barclay examines a patient's teeth; laboratory technician José Gomez painted the mural behind them. La Clinica, funded by the Public Health Service, offers complete *medical* and dental services to needy Chicanos in the city. Chicano fourth-graders in Denver learn to lay out a newspaper at Escuela Tlatelolco, a privately financed school that teaches political activism to the young.

$\mathcal{M}$oonlight bathes the adobe buildings of San Geronimo de Taos, north of Santa Fe. Pueblo Indians for centuries built their terraced villages without openings in the walls, for better defense against enemy tribes; ladders gave access to openings in the roofs. Resisting the white man's influence, most Taos Indians choose to live without telephones, electricity, or running water. Thousands of summer tourists, however, constitute a major source of income —including "modeling fees" for photographs. Crucita Romera takes freshly baked bread from an outdoor beehive oven, a form borrowed from the Spanish; she often sells bread in the village curio shop. Her mother-in-law, after decades of meeting inquisitive strangers in steadily rising numbers, granted an off-season photographer a single pose.

*S*ummer festival on the Blackfeet Reservation in Montana draws Indian and tourist alike. In a shelter on the powwow grounds, Blackfeet play an ancient ceremonial gambling game with sticks and bones. In former days, players from different tribes competed for beads, horses, and other valuables. Today dancers vie for prizes of money and blankets. Eyes closed in concentration, a woman tape-records drum music while boys display their skill and two young girls await their turn.

*E*mphatic — and unofficial, a small sign at the edge of the Taos Reservation warns trespassers off Indian lands. Such intrusions increase as the scenery and healthful climate of the Rockies draw growing numbers of dissatisfied people away from urban areas. Fred Hopman (above) built his solar-heated house at nearby Arroyo Seco five years ago. Summer resident Dennis Luftig, romping with his family as a June day wanes, tosses his young son into the air.

A PORTFOLIO OF MOUNTAIN FLORA

Wheeler Peak

E STARTED in the desert, down among the gritty haunts of rattlers, and ended in fields of snow going rotten under the breath of spring. We dodged spiny cactus and stroked the smooth bark of birch. We traded heat for cold, exhaustion for giddiness at the heights. We climbed a mountain.

Not climbed, really—no technical maneuvers with ropes and the magical little widgets of protection; rather we drove and walked, the three of us, through a catalogue of Rocky Mountain floral life.

The mountain was Wheeler, the highest in New Mexico at 13,161 feet and one that carries a full inventory of ecological zones, from desert sagebrush to alpine tundra. Rising near Taos, Wheeler Peak is round and kind to those who follow its paths past timberline, up to where pieces of cloud hang in the air like tapestries of fleece.

I went with Dr. William C. Martin, a professor of biology at the University of New Mexico, and Warren Wagner, a graduate student there. It was a day in early June when we set out by car from Taos. The temperature near the Rio Grande canyon was in the 80's, and the air was too thick and stationary to stir the desert grasses. Jackrabbits scurried among the sagebrush and the soapweed.

Dr. Martin's hay fever was bothering him, and he said he looked forward to getting up on Wheeler Peak for relief in the thin, clear air. He is a short, stocky, balding man, a native of Kentucky who has been on the university faculty for nearly twenty years. His field is botany, and his focus of interest the flora of New Mexico. He has been to the top of Wheeler Peak many times, always with his eyes trained on the life that springs from the soil.

Warren Wagner is Martin's assistant. Slender and bearded, he is working for an advanced degree in biology. Like Martin, he has

Wild columbine—protected as Colorado's state flower—springs from a shaded slope on Aspen Mountain. It flourishes in aspen groves throughout the Rockies' higher reaches, grows sparingly from foothill to timberline.

browsed extensively over the slopes during previous climbs, but when we started walking, his stride revealed the enthusiasm of discovery.

In this area a desert life zone extends to about 6,500 feet above sea level. A path we took was wide, but steep. Martin and Wagner walked briskly, pausing here and there to venture into the fields. The blazing star, a night bloomer, lay in the bright sunlight with its lemon-colored petals hidden in the embrace of leaves rough as sandpaper. Desert marigolds wove patterns in white and orange.

We moved into woodland as the wind, marbled now with chill, began to gust. A dog appeared and joined us, taking to the path with a gait that was at once haughty and, to one by this time counting each breath as a blessing, contemptuous. He was of mixed breed—mostly shepherd, I think—and his black and white coat was pleated with burrs. His oversized paws gave him a touch of the clown when he left the path for a closer examination of the trees—piñon and juniper and oaks, giving sparse shade to a cover of grasses and shrubs.

"This is the one-seed juniper," Martin said. "It's common in New Mexico. In other places, the juniper usually has two to four seeds in the cone." The oaks were scrubby at this elevation, but the beargrass stood tall with the white flowers packed like cones on the tufted stalks. Our companion, the dog, tasted one, or rather his lolling tongue flapped against one of the flowers as he passed. Not all of the beargrass held color, for this member of the lily family may go as long as seven years without flowering.

We watched for animals, but saw none. They were there, though— black bear and mule deer, and bighorns (reintroduced in 1965) and beaver and others. Mountain lions have hunted on Wheeler Peak, and as recently as January 1974 a little boy was killed by one near the town of Espanola, some sixty miles south.

Above 7,000 feet, trees had replaced many of the shrubs and dominated the landscape. For the next 2,000 feet, the mountain carried ponderosa pine, Douglas fir, aspen, and more juniper. Of all of those, the ponderosa pine was the most prevalent, although thinning out as we moved higher toward the last zone before the timberline. Happily, the dog was tiring, as we all were, and his movements no longer mocked the frailties of man. He was off the path now, back in a field among the orange-red bursts of Indian paintbrush. And there were candytufts back there, too, showing white in the sunshine.

Dr. Martin announced that his hay fever was no longer bothering him; the air was fresh, and too thin to carry the ticklish demons of sneeze. He pointed to a New Mexico maple just starting to bud and said, "That one is sure taking its time coming out." He approached another tree and beckoned me over. "Feel the bark," he said. It was soft and spongy. "That's a corkbark fir. It has a shorter life than the Douglas, and you find it with spruce—mostly between 9,000 and 10,800 feet."

Here the mountain was serving its most lavish feast of growth. The trees—fir and spruce and aspen—were thickly clustered, and the clearings were matted with herbage and shrubs. Streamers of sunlight did little to ward off the cold that had settled in. "We're going to run into a lot of snow before long," Martin said, looking with some skepticism at the sneakers he was wearing. The dog, however, was undaunted, plunging ahead with newfound energy as if someone had hurled a stick to the very summit and commanded "fetch."

Most of the aspens we saw were young—35 to 40 years—as trees go, but for an aspen at this altitude, nearly a lifetime. They had come in after a fire, the first tree to reclaim the charred land. But at one spot a snowslide had left fallen trees all around.

"The fibers of the aspen snap easily," Martin told me, "and that's one reason why the wood is not well suited for building purposes."

ow we reached the last ecological zone before the alpine tundra. This is a coniferous forest, sometimes called the spruce-fir association, and it ranges up to 12,000 feet. The dwarf juniper reached out to cover a wide area, while the . mountain lover, an evergreen shrub highly tolerant of shade, crowded around the base of many of the trees. The bearberry was in flower— dainty blossoms like tiny pink jugs.

Wagner stopped and lowered himself to his knees. Gently, he cupped a flower in one hand—a flower so slender and delicate as to suggest that angels had tended this garden. "The twinflower," he said. Rising from its base of evergreen that trailed off in many directions, the flowers, always in pairs, were pink and white, and they had about them a sweet fragrance.

We ventured off the path, back into a clearing, and marveled at the growth. I came upon a wild strawberry plant at 11,000 feet, still small but leafy, with the promise of flowering within a month. I crushed a piece of fernlike yarrow—used by Indians for medicinal purposes— and the smell was that of turpentine. There were rocks covered with tightly-clinging saxifrage, and in other places the ground gave up blueberry and fireweed.

A log lay in the field, so we sat on it, saying nothing. Even the dog sensed the tenor of that moment, sprawling at our feet with his head cradled on a patch of yellow mustard flowers. Martin and Wagner scanned the area, alert to any growth unknown to them. Up ahead, the path took a sharp turn, and once we rounded that, we knew, the timberline would not be far away. Also, the snow would be there.

As we again started out, we saw, for the first time on Wheeler Peak, the lichen known as old-man's-beard. It hung on the limbs of a spruce in clumps, like Spanish moss, gray and willowy. Nearby was a bog, watered by the overflow of a stream driven to frenzy by snow melt. "It's still a little too early for the bog to be at its best," Martin said. "In another month, it will be fantastic."

Even now it was the showplace of the life zone. White-flowering marsh marigolds with bright yellow centers grew all along the banks of the stream—some enthusiasts gather the buds for salad, but luckily none had come here. The white flowers of the elderberry lay clustered on hollow, pithy stems, while the whitlow grass dusted the bog with gold, as buttercups do in a meadow.

It was ahead now, no more than 100 yards away: the snow. Already it lay in patches, thick where the shade fell. The tree line was perhaps 500 feet away, and beyond that another 1,500 feet or so of tundra to the top. The wind had force enough to make each step forward a definite effort. "It's not going to be easy from here on," Martin said.

We rested. The dog rolled in the snow, like a health faddist just out of the sauna, while Wagner tried to identify a small flower that pushed through the slush at his feet. He studied it from various angles.

"An orchid of some kind," he concluded, turning to look a final time at the flower as we continued on, nearing the tree line. Snow cover made it obvious that we were too early for most of the alpine tundra flora. Winter was still in attendance in the last zone, as it would be, Martin estimated, for another month.

Still, the tundra was spotted here and there with the miracle of growth. I saw alpine willow, rising no more than a few inches from the ground. Rushes and sedges were reclaiming snow-melt areas. And the snow would continue to retreat, giving the thin layer of soil over to an amazing variety of plants: sandwort and forget-me-nots, chick-weed and campion, phlox and clover. And much more.

Of the more than nine million square miles of tundra in the Northern Hemisphere, nearly half is alpine. And this was part of it: the treeless stretch of shallow soil, whipped by winds and buried in snow except for a brief period each year—but a period packed by nature with a colorful festival of life.

The ascent ended with the snow above our shoes (not only above, but *in* Dr. Martin's sneakers). When we turned, the wind at our backs pushed us into a semi-trot. Soon we were back among the trees—but not before I spotted an alpine sunflower, the old-man-of-the-mountain, and early-blooming fleabane with flowers as purple as a lilac.

The cold trailed off and we shed our jackets. And suddenly I remembered the times when, as a child, I climbed out of the cool caverns of the ice company's delivery truck (chased out, I was) to feel the immediate warmth of a summer day. Past the aspens we went, and down, looking back and feeling good for having been up there. The dog followed us to the bottom where he sniffed at a shrub, turned, and headed back for the spruce.

DODECATHEON PULCHELLUM

*Plants of moist earth and cool air, shooting stars mark the
twisting courses of streams from the heights to the valleys.*

Above the dark gorge cut by the Rio Grande, a prickly pear finds roothold; beyond, Wheeler Peak rises above the plain. Hedgehog cactus, with its waxy red blossoms, and Indian paintbrush can survive on such arid slopes and mesas. Utah named the white sego lily its state flower: Mormon pioneers escaped famine by eating its bulbs, as the Indians did.

CALOCHORTUS NUTTALLII

OPUNTIA POLYCANTHA

CASTILLEJA SP.   ECHINOCEREUS TRIGLOCHIDIATUS

Quaking aspens shimmer around scattered evergreens, robing Smuggler Mountain in golden hues while oaks redden for autumn. Beneath a rising moon, arrowleaf balsamroot nods on a high meadow, where a careless step might release the pungent odor of pink wild onion blooms. Aptly named bearberry, also called kinnikinnik, forms part of the diet of birds and browsing animals as well as black or grizzly bears. Spines of the elk thistle protect its delicate bud.

ALLIUM GEYERI

BALSAMORHIZA SAGITTATA

POPULUS TREMULOIDES

ARCTOSTAPHYLOS UVA-URSI

CIRISIUM COLORADENSE

ERYTHRONIUM GRANDIFLORUM

KALMIA POLIFOLIA

Yellow for caution, the avalanche lily springs from subalpine slopes—in special abundance near melting snowbanks on moraines. But it blooms too late in spring to warn unwary climbers who ascend so far. An evergreen of the subalpine zone, dew-misted swamp laurel thrives in bogs or on mossy streambanks. Still higher, old-man-of-the-mountain crests a windswept ridge. Short stems and overall dwarfing characterize such plants of the alpine tundra. Unlike true sunflowers, this does not turn its head to follow the sun's course through the day; it faces eastward, toward dawn.

JILL DURRANCE (UPPER AND LOWER LEFT)

HYMENOXYS GRANDIFLORA

CHAPTER FIVE

Ranching: A Rugged Business

BUT FOR THE COMPASSION of a trainman, Allyn O'Hair might never have reached Paradise Valley. Probably the times had something to do with it, for the year was 1930, and the depression tended to give rise to mutual understanding of the problems of economic survival.

"Have you got a ticket?" The voice was sharp, cold, almost menacing. O'Hair, exhausted from having jogged along the tops of a string of boxcars, looked around. He was in the caboose, alone except for the stern-faced guardian of the rails.

"No, sir, I don't have a ticket. I'm being sent C.O.D."

Forty-five years later, Allyn O'Hair sat at a table in the dining room of his house and recalled that the trainman allowed him to remain aboard. "He didn't bother me at all. When the train got to Livingston, I got off. I remember that it was 30 below zero outside. I got a train to Brisbin, and then walked to the ranch."

He had done a summer's haying there, and was taken on again as a hand. Not too many years passed before he married the owner's daughter. And now he owns the ranch.

In my judgment, there are few more appealing valleys in the Rockies than Paradise. Veined by the Yellowstone River, this strong land carries northward into Montana from the bounds of Yellowstone National Park. The O'Hair ranch covers nearly 20,000 acres.

As a rancher, Allyn O'Hair is involved in the activity with the most impact on the well-being of agriculture in the Mountain West. It is a business of deep uncertainty. Each year is a gamble, and a bad year is full of pain. Weather, disease, and market fluctuations are among the forces by which fortunes rise and fall.

Ranching in the Rockies means, most of all, the raising and selling of cattle. It requires vast amounts of land, and, for anyone just

"When I've got water, I can make most any crop grow," says Allyn O'Hair, who raises alfalfa on his family ranch in Montana's Paradise Valley. To bring in water, the ranch's founder dug a 15-mile canal a century ago.

starting in the business, capital resources of equal scope. Most young men who operate cattle spreads in the mountains today are beneficiaries of inheritance. So it is likely to be with O'Hair's sons.

"Even though I get discouraged at times," he said, "I always tell my two sons, 'Look, your great-grandparents came here and they made a living in the cow business, and if we take care of it right and watch it carefully, we should be able to make a living too.'"

Nothing, I believe, is more symbolic of the Mountain West than the cattle ranch. Its fences line the highway—mile after mile of taut wire snapping across the broad, grassy seas of pasture. The land is without trees except where a cluster of cottonwoods drops shade on the ranch house; and that's back a mile, maybe two, at the end of a dirt road on which a pickup truck raises pirouettes of dust.

Most of the cattle are Hereford, a breed developed in England. Henry Clay was among the first importers of Herefords into this country, around 1817. Now, they graze throughout the Mountain West, bivouacked in the pastures with white faces pushed to the grass, forever eating to add bulk to the blocky reddish bodies.

The Aberdeen Angus is there in large numbers, too: smooth-coated and polled, it matches the blackness of its shadow until it appears in distant fields like an outcropping of coal. Also to be found on ranches in the Rockies are the Shorthorn and the more recently imported "exotic breeds," such as Simmental and Charolais.

But one breed, more than any other, was responsible for styling this region as cow country. It carried neither the bulk nor the stumpiness of the Angus. Its movements were swift and tireless, and there was little docility to its nature. It was lean and wild.

It came from Mexico and Texas, and it was called the Longhorn.

ONGHORNS FIRST APPEARED in the Rockies in the mid-19th century, when there was a demand for beef to feed the gold prospectors. It was not the best of beef by today's standards, for the Longhorn fed on nothing but grass and other wild forage. These were steaks with little marbling—chewy and stringy and sometimes invested with wild onion. It was fresh beef, though, and to a miner weary of jackrabbit and jerky, it was delicious.

For about three decades, the Longhorn ranged over the West, and the image of the gaunt animal running before a lasso was etched and hung in the dream gallery of millions who shared a fantasy of a new life beyond the Mississippi. Still, as a flesh-and-blood machine geared to transform grass into beef, the Longhorn was somewhat of a failure. To improve the quality of the meat, the animal was crossed with other breeds. And with the dropping of calves in succeeding years, there was a corresponding erosion of the Longhorn's characteristics until little remained. The steak was better, yes, and the income, but the West had been drained of some vivid color.

Trends in the cattle business are such now that the Longhorn may be making a modest comeback.

"In 1974, we lost $100 a head on everything we put in the feedlots," O'Hair said. "Ranchers by the score went broke that year. Feed got awfully high, and cattle prices went all to pieces."

In that year of economic hardship (by contrast, cattle prices the preceding year had reached new highs), 37 million cattle were slaughtered in the United States. Of that number, 24 million were put through feedlots. There the beast is fattened on grain to add flavor and marbling to the beef; and, of course, to ensure that the animal will not go to slaughter with less than ideal weight. Weight at the time of entry onto the feedlot is between 400 and 800 pounds; between 180 and 200 days later, when the last meal is in the ruminant mixer, the weight is up to half-a-ton or thereabouts.

Because of the high cost of feed, and a recent change in the U. S. Department of Agriculture's quality-grading system for beef (less marbling needed for Prime or Choice rating), there are movements in the Mountain West today toward more reliance on grass.

In 1975, for the first time in the 69-year history of the National Western Stock Show at Denver, there were Longhorns up for sale. The word was being passed: a hardy breed; adapted to adverse weather; without need for grains and other specialized feeds.

It's not that the Longhorn is likely to reclaim the range from the Hereford, because, for one thing, there are probably no more than 10,000 registered cows of the breed in all of the world. Rather, through crossbreeding, the Longhorn can impart some of its self-sufficiency to the Hereford and the Angus.

"The purebred cattle industry has been in a rut." Don Vaniman swung in his chair as he gave the assessment, a tall man with the stamp of the Mountain West on his dress and speech. "For 40 years it put too much value on short, blocky cattle. What's needed is a taller, faster-growing animal, an animal that feeds mostly on forage."

That animal, he said, is the Simmental.

Vaniman is executive secretary of the American Simmental Association, with headquarters in Bozeman, Montana. There are 8,000 members, he said, with new ones being added each year.

Simmentals began to appear on ranches in the Rockies in 1967, following centuries of popularity in Europe. In Switzerland, for example, the breed accounts for 47 percent of the cattle population, in Austria, 70 percent. And of more than 106 million head of cattle in the Soviet Union, 16 million are Simmental.

"Now, the average Simmental herd size in this country is 246," Vaniman said. "They feed on roughage, and they grow rapidly. And they're never overly fat. It takes only two-tenths of an inch of fat for taste and preservative; anything over that has to be trimmed by the packer. We're trying to put the cow business on a more scientific basis by keeping close records of the performance of the animals and sharing this computerized information with our members."

There are many ranchers in the Mountain West who keep good records and seek improved performance, but who dismiss the possibility of such exotic breeds as the Simmental making serious inroads in the cattle business. Jess Kilgore is not one.

His ranch sits in Montana's Madison Valley, east of the Tobacco Root Mountains. It is small as cattle spreads go in the Mountain West — only 5,000 acres — but the operation is so finely tuned to efficiency that size seems of less importance. Owner of the ranch since 1957,

Jess Kilgore has set new standards for high performance by a herd. His cattle have been Simmental since 1969.

"Economic pressures demanded that we in the cattle business do something with added value if we were to survive," he said. "So in the 1960's I started performance testing in my cattle to evaluate a breeding animal as precisely as possible. Traditionally, the cattle industry rated an animal on its standing in shows—how it looks."

Kilgore records such details as the number of pounds a nursing calf gains each day, weight added in the pasture, and the size of the pelvic arch. His herd is indexed, analyzed, and computer coded. So it is with other Simmental herds. With such information available to members of the Association, it is simply a matter of consulting readouts to match animals for breeding—95 percent of Simmental breeding in the United States is by artificial insemination.

"To achieve all of this," Kilgore told me, "we worked with experts in universities, with the U. S. Department of Agriculture, and so forth. We were determined to find a better way to raise cattle, and we did. So now we have an animal that takes much less grain, and yet we're weaning calves here on this ranch that weigh 600 pounds

Mules provide muscle to raise the wooden fork of a haystacker; when the hay drops onto the pile, men spread it evenly. The O'Hair ranch relied on stackers until the 1930's, when balers replaced them.

instead of the 400 pounds in other breeds. And that kind of efficient weight gain continues to maturity of the animal. The Simmental is by far the most successful exotic breed in the United States."

I walked among the stock on Kilgore's ranch and found animals that stood tall and muscular. Some were yellowish brown, others dark red with white markings. Docile in nature, they accepted my close presence with hardly a stir other than swishing of tails.

I T WAS COLD that day, and the mountains were tinted purple, as if bruised by the wind that pushed through the valley. Later, in the nearby town of Three Forks, in a bar where the tables were patterned with the glossy, sticky stain of dried beer, I overheard speculation on what the approaching weather would be like.

It would be a mild winter.

It would be one hell of a winter.

It would be a winter of such heavy snows that roofs would collapse and roads would be closed until spring.

It would be a winter of grace, with a thaw in February.

As it happened, the winter was cruel. As a result of just one blizzard in calving season, on March 27 of 1975, an estimated 15,000 head of cattle died in Colorado. For many miles, covering thousands of acres, the scene was one of tragedy. A calf with eyes open, as if alive and inquisitive, lay where it fell, frozen to death at the age of three days. And there were others—calves, cows, and yearlings—all about, struck down in the bloodless massacre of the winter wind.

Who has not seen the picture in any of a thousand books with the West as a subject: the cow drifting with the storm to its back, head lowered, hide crusted with ice and snow, calf at its side. . . .

None of the pains of ranching is so severe as the cruelty of weather, especially as it affects supplies of water. Cowmen have gone to their death fighting over claims to water. To the rancher in the Mountain West, the land is valuable in terms of water—water measured as covering one acre one foot deep, water that feeds down from the mountains, bearing the chill of the snow that it was, to join rivers that drain thousands upon thousands of square miles of the states that carry the Continental Divide.

In all of the controversy over industrial expansion in the Mountain West, nothing is cited more often than the effect on resources of fresh water. How much water will the coal and oil shale industry require? And, equally important, how serious is the danger of pollution? Indeed, in assessing crimes against earth, those with whom I talked about the present and future availability of water in the mountain states reserved their harshest judgment for the abuse of this most precious of natural resources. To litter the ground, they said, is irresponsible, and to foul the air we breathe is contemptible. But to kill a stream—to squeeze the life from it until suckers replace the trout—to do that, they agreed, is insane.

Just as water has coursed through the history of the Mountain West, giving shape and direction to many important events, so has it always epitomized the dignity of nature there. For some this means a river with white water of rage. For others it's a skinny, silvery stream that winds down a mountain. And for youngsters living in Denver and Salt Lake City and Boise, like youngsters in cities everywhere, the best comes after a summer storm, when ships made of sticks and things can sail with the tide in gutter seas.

Allyn O'Hair will give you a rancher's evaluation.

"We use about 2,000 miner's inches of water just for irrigation on this ranch," he said. "A cubic foot of water running at the rate of a foot per second is 40 miner's inches. It was the miners who came in and settled, and they applied for water to operate their mines, and this is the measurement they adopted. There'd be a whole bunch of prospectors on one little creek and each wanted some water. So they agreed that each would build a little box and let the water run through that and be measured.

"Primarily, we get our water from the Yellowstone River, but we also get some out of Trail Creek. Now let me tell you some more about the water because it means everything. When the man who started this ranch settled here, he realized that the use of water was the life-blood of the country. He had to have water if he was going to stay here and be a success in the ranching business. So he started to build a canal by which he could take water from the Yellowstone."

O'Hair paused, rose from his chair and walked to a window to look out over the seemingly endless reach of his acreage. Somewhere out there his two sons were starting the drive of a thousand cattle to summer pasture. First, the calves had been branded.

"He and a surveyor friend started building that canal with teams and scrapers," he continued. "They worked for ten years on that ditch before they ever got a drop of water. Every fall he'd get his cattle together and ship them off to Chicago. After he got his money for the cattle, he'd pay his bills and spend what was left over on that ditch. When he ran out of money, he'd let the work go until the next year, when he sold more cattle.

"That was my wife's grandfather, O. T. Armstrong, and I think what he did was a study in perseverance. That ditch is still in operation—not only that, but it now serves the whole valley."

There was a time, I learned, when there was more hay grown on the O'Hair ranch than in all the rest of the valley, simply because of the availability of water through the canal. The other ranches had only creeks to draw on, and they often went dry in the summer.

"Water to agriculture out here is everything," O'Hair said. "Well, not everything exactly, but it's certainly the most important thing. Of course, there is a need for energy, too, to run the tractors and so on. The ranchers say they have to have the water, and there are others who say the water is needed to go through a dam and produce energy. It's a dilemma."

Since 1964 there have been plans on file for a dam to be constructed on the Yellowstone, in Paradise Valley. If that comes to pass, the O'Hair ranch will be flooded, as will most of the valley.

Controversy over the potential dam has been intense and heated. The ranchers, of course, fear that if it comes to a choice between water for them and water for a hydroelectric plant in a time of drought, they will lose; and they think the probability of drought has been underestimated in the planning — at Paradise Valley and elsewhere.

Water resources are a matter for the Bureau of Reclamation, which has no current studies for Paradise Valley but has come under fire over water policy elsewhere in the Rockies. Opponents point to what has happened along the Bighorn River, at Bighorn Lake and at Boysen Reservoir. The bureau is selling water rights for energy development, an action being challenged in court through a suit filed by conservation organizations, individuals, groups that rely on particular irrigation facilities, and the State of Montana.

The plaintiffs charge that the bureau has awarded contracts to corporations for more water than could be supplied in a bad year. "These contracts were signed between 1967 and 1971, many of them with oil companies," said Katherine Fletcher of the Denver office of the Environmental Defense Fund. "Congress meant this water to be used for agriculture, not for the energy industry.

"The bureau was established for the purpose of irrigating the West," Miss Fletcher continued. "But now it's changing its emphasis in the Upper Missouri drainage — to water for strip-mined coal.

"It's like the government's retaining the mineral rights on grazing lands, in the Stock-Raising Homestead Act of 1916. That was done to prevent mining companies from setting up dummy ranches just to get the minerals. Strip mining was not in question then, and mine shafts wouldn't ruin much land for grazing. But now the government is selling its mineral rights to companies that will do strip mining.

"Paradise Valley, you see, raises larger questions than water. It involves the whole idea of developing the West."

IN A REGION where agencies of the federal government hold brawny clout, the Bureau of Land Management stands as a heavyweight. For one thing, it manages much of the public land on which livestock is allowed to graze — for a fee paid by the rancher. This, too, is a point of controversy, for the bureau's critics charge that overgrazing has damaged the land. Indeed, the bureau has conceded that its management of rangeland is plagued with shortcomings. Its practices vary from state to state; but in one survey conducted by a team of its own resource managers, it was found, among other things, that grazing allotments were being awarded without consideration for wildlife.

It has also fallen to the bureau to protect wild horses on public lands in the Mountain West, and that too has drawn the wrath of many. The herd south of Challis, Idaho, illustrates this matter of concern to land managers and ranchers. In 1974, there were 353 horses in the herd; a year later, the count was up to 407. The increase continues at a rate of about 28 percent annually.

Public Law 86-234 forbids the use of motorized vehicles in capturing the animals. A horseback roundup is still permissible, but too slow and costly to be effective. So ranchers complain that wild horses are now competing with livestock for food, to the extent of disrupting the natural plant succession and thus hastening erosion.

In many ways, the issue of the wild horses reveals what seems to be at times the one unbridgeable gulf between the environmentalist and the person whose fortune is tied to the land. The former, perhaps, sees the wild horse as a magnificent creature, more likely than not posed on a distant butte, mane ruffled by the wind, head high, spirit soaring, free. The rancher is no less appreciative of the beauty of an unbridled stallion, but the animal, he feels, is a threat to his livelihood. With the passage of such laws as 86-234, he knows he is losing the battle, and he knows too that the biggest guns are trained on him from Washington.

"Yes, we have weather hazards and disease among the cattle and a lot of other things, but let me tell you that our biggest worry is the government," Allyn O'Hair said. "We can figure out these other things and take our chances with them, but you can never tell what the government is going to do. Regulations, price controls — the harassments never stop. There used to be a time when you could operate a ranch without public interference. No more. You can't do anything now without the public having a voice in it. They want to regulate your water and your land.

"They want you to take your cattle off the public lands. There's a tremendous amount of frustration, not only because of the federal government but because of the state, too. Whenever the legislature meets, it makes a rancher shake in his boots — you know, because of the laws they can impose on us. And meetings, meetings, meetings — trying to defend yourself and have it so that the other guy is satisfied and you can still make a living."

O LESS BURDENED with problems is the sheep rancher, for the sheepman has the coyote to contend with. Again, it is a government order that has disturbed those who deal in lamb and wool. Because of a federal restriction, sheepmen claim, predator losses are running high.

"Since 1972, the poison used against coyotes has been banned. Only trapping and shooting are permitted, and neither is very effective against the coyote."

Dr. Don Balser, chief of predator damage research for the U. S. Fish and Wildlife Service, in Denver, went on to say, "The coyote population is healthy and expanding. There is a need for selective, safe toxicants to control predators, but they should be used by trained personnel only."

On the west slope of the Rockies in Colorado, there are bands of 800 to 1,200 sheep with only one shepherd. Such odds seem to favor the coyote, but more shepherds would make little difference.

There have been experiments at controlling the predator by means other than poison, none very successful. A repellent was developed, in hopes that when a coyote approached a lamb smelling of the stuff, he would back off in nauseated disgust. Certain lambs in a herd were sprayed, and a coyote came in and made a kill. Alas, the victim was one of the scented.

The coyote has its defenders, persons who argue that the decline in sheep numbers should be laid to causes other than federal restrictions on predator control. After all, they point out, it had continued for thirty years before the ban. The popularity of synthetic fibers has

Machine age, 1920: A steam engine powers a belt-driven thresher. Paradise Valley ranchers rented the steamer from its owner and drove it from spread to spread at harvest time. A wagon tank supplies water to the boiler.

diminished the demand for wool. Profit margins on lamb have long been uncertain. Moreover, they say, some of the killings blamed on coyotes may well be the work of domestic dogs gone wild.

Certainly a shortage of workers—specifically, Basque shepherds —has aggravated the hardships of a troubled industry.

For many years, Basque sheepmen were brought to ranches in the Mountain West from Spain on three-year contracts, with the option of applying for American citizenship thereafter. That flow of labor has now greatly diminished. John Morrison of the American Sheep Producers Council in Denver cites three reasons for that:

A current Labor Department policy to encourage the use of domestic labor—Indians and Mexican-Americans, for example.

Department regulations on shelter for farm laborers—60 square feet per worker, one window or skylight as emergency exit for a room; for summer, effective sanitary facilities, a convenient water supply. (Morrison comments: "Because of the nomadic nature of sheepherding, particularly during the summer when a sheepherder is in a tent or a wagon, these requirements are impossible, indeed ridiculous.")

Better job opportunities and higher standards of living in Spain today. Fewer young Basques want to leave their homeland to work as shepherds in the United States.

I recall, though, how it was when all of the ranch hands on a spread I visited in Idaho were Basque:

It was a February day, and the lambing season had started. The wind was strong, blowing out of a sky still puffy and dark from yesterday's rain. But that was good because the wind would dry the mud in the fields. I watched as a large black horse pulling a cart was led toward a group of several hundred ewes. A Basque walked through the herd, inspecting the animals. Finding one in labor, he quickly separated her from the others, lifted and plopped the 180-pound ewe on her back in the cart. The horse plodded off to a nearby shed, where the ewe could drop the lamb in a bed of straw.

I joined the Basques for lunch. None spoke more than a few words of English. One puzzled over a dentist's bill received in the morning mail until the owner of the ranch, a Basque himself, said he would take care of it. Seated on wooden benches at a long table, the sheepmen from Spain quickly ate their stew and codfish, drank their red wine, and then went back to the fields dried by the wind.

However pressing the problems of economic survival, the rancher today has one valuable asset: his land. With nothing on it—not a cow, or a sheep, or hidden treasures of coal and oil—it is worth a fortune. But for a man like Allyn O'Hair, it is a fortune not likely to be realized. His land increases in value, but revenue from it does not increase accordingly and income does not reflect investment.

"My acreage involves a tremendous amount of money," he said. "We've talked about the possibility of selling out, but I don't know— I don't even like to think about that. When you've put a lifetime in the land, improving it and watching it grow, and watching the improvements that show up sooner or later, it's a pretty dreadful thing to think of selling it and walking away."

Still, more and more ranches are being sold in the mountain states. Many are being purchased for uses other than ranching—recreational development, for example, and industrial activities.

Now under construction on a former ranch near Durango, Colorado, is a 30-million-dollar condominium-recreational facility complex. When completed, it will offer two 18-hole golf courses, four swimming pools, indoor and outdoor tennis courts, arenas for horseback riding, trap and skeet shooting, archery range, ski area, and more. It is all going up on what an official of the complex, called Tamarron, described as "an old cow pasture."

And in the foothills not far from Denver, the Johns-Manville Corporation bought a 10,000-acre ranch for use as its world headquarters. It was a bold move—from the corporate canyons of New York to the shadows of the Rockies. Those 10,000 acres of plains and valleys and rolling hills cost the company nearly eight million dollars.

The Ken-Caryl Ranch, as it is called, was once a producer not only of cattle and sheep, but also of quarter horses. Presidents William Howard Taft and Theodore Roosevelt were entertained there. It was a ranch on the grand scale, with a manor house looking out over the central valley from a knoll. The last owner died in 1963, and the property remained in his estate until Johns-Manville came along in 1971 with the check made out in millions.

Of course, 10,000 acres is a lot of land. There will be housing and recreational developments where, as the company put it, "those who ultimately choose this location as their home or place to work can enjoy all phases of Ken-Caryl activities without infringing on the environment and life-style of others."

During the Civil War a law was passed by Congress, and as a result, land that now sells for many thousands of dollars an acre was free for the taking. This was the Homestead Act of 1862, and it provided that any person who was the head of a family, or 21 years old, an American citizen or applicant for citizenship—and had not borne arms against the government—could stake claim to 160 acres.

There was confusion. And fraud. It might be possible to make a living working 160 acres in the East, but not in the semiarid stretches of the Mountain West. So cattlemen spread their herds over vast reaches of unfenced acreage and dared anyone to move them off. When the fences finally began to appear, there were wars—wars over water, wars over rangeland, wars over the right of a man to use this big and spectacular mountain land as he saw fit.

IOLENCE WAS MOST PREVALENT in Wyoming, where cattle barons held enormous power for many years. It was bad enough for the homesteader to fence his 160 acres, thereby cutting off the access to some water for the cattle, but even worse were the sheep, chomping the grass of the range right down to the roots. They were all fighting—cattleman, homesteader, and sheepman—and there were times of threatened massacre. In 1892 Washington had to order the U. S. cavalry to break up a serious confrontation between owners of small and large ranches in Wyoming's Johnson County. Hired gunmen were involved, but the death toll reached only four before order was restored.

Dynamite and clubs were used to kill thousands of sheep in the Bighorn Basin of Wyoming in an attack carried out by cattlemen who wore masks. That was in the early part of the 20th century, and there would be more attacks and counterattacks in the years to follow.

Wyoming has felt domination by the cattle industry more than any of the other mountain states. Even today there are ten times as many cattle and sheep in the state as human beings. Yet, the number of ranches there is growing smaller.

In 1975, there were 8,100 farms and ranches in the state, down 11 percent within a decade. That doesn't seem like many for a state large enough to hold 80 Rhode Islands, but consider this: The average size of the farm-ranch is 4,438 acres, and growing larger.

The trend across the Mountain West is to consolidation of ranches, the buying out of the smaller by the larger. For only through a large-scale operation is it possible to make a decent living as a cattleman today. Some dealers in exotic breeds are convinced they can reverse the trend by breaking dependency on grain feeding. Perhaps. But meanwhile, the problems mount, including this new one:

Something bizarre is happening on some ranches in the mountains these days. Cattle are being killed and mutilated, and no one seems to know by whom or for what reason. It is baffling because there is often a conspicuous absence of blood, on the ground or in the carcass of the prey. Yet, in almost all instances, the animal's tongue, sexual organs, and udders have been removed.

The work of predators, says Dr. Balser.

Darts—they're shot with darts containing some lethal agent, say some.

Witchcraft, say others, and Satanism; weirdos; and maybe visitors from outer space.

Whatever it is, it's causing concern, because with the cost of raising a cow today it is painful to lose even one. No less troublesome is the rustling. In the same Johnson County of Wyoming where federal troops intervened to stop the range war, ranchers lost so many cattle in 1974 that they hired an investigator of their own.

Lawmen believe that modern-day rustlers use pickup trucks equipped with trailers large enough to hold 15 head of cattle. They approach a herd, erect a fence and drive in as many cattle as they can haul away. Often the theft is amateurish and crude, such as the case of the two women who slaughtered a cow and then pulled it by a rope attached to the bumper of a car for 24 miles. That, in truth, is a far departure from the stubble-bearded gunslingers who swooped down out of the hills on lathered mounts to drive off a whole herd without so much as a whip on a hide.

But times have changed. And Allyn O'Hair sits in the warm dining room of his house and wonders if it's been for the better. Whatever has happened, he continues to enjoy his work. He continues to revel in the beauty of Paradise Valley.

He continues to tell his sons they can make a go of it.

To protect a newborn Hereford from freezing in windswept snow, Allyn's younger son, Andy, carries the 80-pound calf into the warmth of a barn. Brothers Andy and Jerry and their father take turns attending the calving cows "daylight till dark and dark till daylight" throughout March and April.

*S*nowcapped summits of the
Absaroka Range rise beyond the
20,000-acre O'Hair ranch,
where cows wait in a calving pen.
"The harder the weather, the harder
a cowhand's job," says Jerry;
here he feeds hay to range cattle
after spending the night caring for
the "drop bunch"—the cows
about to give birth.

Cow's milk fed from a baby bottle nourishes a whiteface calf abandoned by its mother. After several feedings revive the orphan, Andy will put it with

a cow whose own calf has died. As a result of the O'Hairs' precautions, 90 percent of their calf crop survives— a high yield in a business subject to the special hazards of mountain storms. Relaxed in a saddle, Andy's five-year-old daughter, Bobbi Jo, enjoys her favorite pastime—watching her father.

Back in the saddle after the long winter, the O'Hairs drive the herd to summer pasture. Cowpunching in the rain soils the chaps and slicker of Andy's wife, Karen. Todd grimaces at the odor of singed hair as he helps his father, Andy, hold down a calf for branding by his grandfather. They can brand, castrate, dehorn, and vaccinate a calf in 30 seconds.

*S*praying life into the land, a center pivot sprinkler—here being adjusted by Jerry—stretches 1,550 feet and slowly swings in a circle to water almost 200 acres. One of three sprinklers on the O'Hair ranch, this model breaks apart for relocation on other fields. When he purchased them, Allyn O'Hair hoped that an increased yield per acre would justify the enormous cost of the systems—usually used for plains irrigation. Today the sprinklers enable the O'Hairs to feed 400 cattle on land that previously supported only 40. Ironically, water—the ranching valley's lifeblood—may bring about its destruction. Residents fear that the water-hungry coal industry and rising demands for hydroelectric generators will encourage building of the Allenspur Dam across the Yellowstone River. The dam would flood much of the valley and end its century-old way of life. Throughout the Rockies, water allocation has become a major issue. Where six-guns once cracked in wars over water rights, opponents now trade legal briefs in a long-term struggle that will decide the economic future of the Mountain West.

*G*asoline power lets one man do the work of 15 on the O'Hair ranch today. A self-propelled bale wagon, with Jerry at the wheel, stacks 3,000 bales of hay a day. Andy hammers the sicklebar of the "swather," or haycutter, into position. Allyn, wiping his brow, prepares a secondhand combine for the barley harvest. Though Jerry serves as ranch mechanic, all hands must know how to run the machinery and make repairs.

*E*mployees join the family when the O'Hairs gather for a Sunday dinner of roast beef, with tossed salad and homemade raisin-cream pie. Meals offer the ranchers one of their few chances to relax. "We make our work our vacation," explains Allyn, who, like the rest of the family, manages fewer than four days off a year. After the feast, Jerry's children, Julie and Justin, savor a second dessert, licking leftover whipped cream. Four grandchildren of Allyn and Agnes O'Hair roam the ranch learning to ride and to care for the animals. Their great-great-grandfather helped build the one-room school where Todd studies second-grade lessons—just as his father, grandmother, and great-grandfather did before him.

"*This land and our family grew up together,*" *reflects Agnes. "The land's in our blood and our hearts are in the land." Her grandson Justin sits near her. In the living room of his home, Todd gets pointers on branding from his father. Changing watch during calving, Andy shares a few thoughts with his father. Despite their lifetimes of hard work, all on the ranch echo the sentiments of Agnes when she says, "Everything considered, there's no place I'd rather be."*

A PORTFOLIO OF
WILDERNESS IN WINTER

Yellowstone

How MANY YEARS have passed since I last stood here on the rim of Old Faithful? Four, maybe five. It was in August, I know, of a summer gone blowsy under the press of heat. The rivers had fallen and slowed, and the brush on the floors of the pine forests had dried until it crackled under step.

I remember too that several thousand tourists stood with me to watch as the famed geyser erupted—hissing, steaming, jetting high off the enduring earth-fires of creation in Yellowstone National Park. Now, but for the presence of a moose (a bilious old bull), I am here alone to marvel at the thermal display; alone because this queen of national parks is locked in snow and silence and all the splendid wrath of Rocky Mountain winter.

Snow stopped falling sometime during the night, ending a two-day storm. The temperature is probably 20 below. Yes, at least that, because the air is like steel, chilling my lungs with every breath. Yet not far away, in a meadow freighted with snow five feet deep, there's an unfrozen pond. The water is gray and stilled and warmed by the heat of Yellowstone's infernal chemistry.

Resting motionless on the water, as if sculpted in ice, is one of the two score trumpeter swans in the park. I watch until there is movement: a curling of the long neck followed by a flash of preening. Soon, with wings chopping through the frozen air, the great bird rises, circles the meadow and speaks to the morning in a brassy voice.

No matter that many animals have migrated to winter feeding grounds elsewhere in the Mountain West—Yellowstone in this season is a festival of wildlife. Tracks in the snow chart the wanderings of elk and bison, moose and coyote. Bighorn sheep are down from the blizzardy upper reaches of the Washburn Range, in the north-central

Cold winter air enhances the morning spectacle of steam billowing from Castle Geyser in Yellowstone National Park. The steam follows an eruption of boiling water, heated by molten rock far underground.

area of the park. Pine martens are preying on squirrels and mice in the long shadows of the lodgepole pines. Eagles are hunched on high branches, at rest between dives on trout in the rivers.

And other predators are stalking the ailing—a bull elk among them.

Once, I suppose, he was an animal of strength and pride and feisty spirit. Age is upon him now. For two days he has been camped on the warm turf at a geyser. Seldom moving, he no longer feeds. Instead, he waits for death. It will come soon.

Coyotes are in attendance. Rather than attack, they will wait until the animal is dead before starting to feed, before ripping into flesh already heavily scarred in the internecine battles of the rut. Maybe that's it. Maybe the elk was once lord of a large harem, commanding the cows of his choice at mating time. And when that ended—when he could no longer triumph over the challenges from younger bulls— he seized on the pursuit of death as the final expression of bravery.

Nobility! Perhaps that's what we look for in the death of a wild animal. If we don't find it, we invent it.

(I returned to the geyser the next day. The elk had moved about twenty yards away from the warm ground to die in the snow. Surprisingly, there were few signs of scavenger feeding on the now-frozen carcass.)

I PUSH THROUGH THE SNOW on cross-country skis. Being new to the sport, I gambol when I'm supposed to glide. My kick turns never quite make it. My poling is a mockery of coordination. Somehow, though, I cover ground. A buffalo—no, bison—stands in my path, a shaggy tank of a beast with no inclination to move. Stopping, thank the Lord, is my high suit in skiing.

The bison's massive head is lowered, swinging back and forth, like a demolition ball, to clear a path to the flattened, yellowed remains of last summer's grass. The scene is invested with symbolism: of a time long past when this hardy animal filled the West with its presence; when the thunder of a spooked herd rivaled that of the heavens.

More than that, the symbolism is of man's excesses and the resulting near-extinction of the bison.

Roderick Hutchinson, a Park Service geologist, is waiting for me at Norris Geyser Basin. By now the weather has turned bad, with wind dropping the chill factor to more than 25 below. There's no horizon, no delineation of sky and earth, no visibility. I seem to be trapped in a hamper full of dingy gray sheets.

Considering Hutchinson's good cheer and exuberance, it might be a day of sunshine and balmy warmth. He's smiling and inviting me to enter this thermal fairyland of ice and steam and creamy mudpots.

Norris is the hottest geyser basin in the world. In winter, nature stages one of its grandest shows here. The underground plumbing is forever at work, flushing rockets of scalding water from the earth. Ice blocks take grotesque shape where the spray falls. Bubbles of mud swell and, *blup*, burst. Beds of algae, rank with color, cling to rocks.

Rick Hutchinson takes delight in it all. "Do you know," he says, "that the thermal areas on just the east side of the Continental Divide release a total of 840 million calories of heat every second?" I am amazed, although in truth I am uncertain how much heat is in a calorie (the burn of a match? the feel of a sick puppy's nose?).

I walk through a veil of steam and savor the warmth. There are rocks at my feet, all slimy with algae. Getting down for a closer look, I see mites and spiders and flies, none larger than a pea. They are thriving, but of course they stay close to the warm algae; in this weather, a flight of more than a few inches away will result in immediate death by freezing. My attention is drawn to a single brown fly, a female consumed with the business of laying eggs. Will she, like the salmon, meet death soon after giving birth?

She will not, apparently. The pink mass of eggs is on the rock, and the fly is staying within the safety zone of warmth. I cannot recall ever having observed the miracle of life in sharper focus.

The buzz I hear is not that of flies, but of approaching snowmobiles. So others have breached the fastness of the park on this winter day. Indeed, before long I watch as two dozen of the squatty machines pass along a road.

And now some young people of rude good health are emerging from the woods on cross-country skis, having been in the back country for as long as a week. Clearly, there's some truth in the Yellowstone Park Company's puffery about "the national park that came out of hibernation."

The company, a private firm, operates sleeping and eating facilities in the park. In 1971 it decided to keep a lodge and some cabins open for use in the winter. That was a sound decision; the occupancy rate has consistently been high and on the increase.

There are three ways to get to the heart of Yellowstone in winter: snowcoach, skis, snowmobile. Most visitors enter by snowmobile. They often come as clubs, with insignia emblazoned on jackets. Seldom does a snowmobiler travel alone here, for the danger of breaking down and being stranded in the unmerciful weather is too great. To ensure human safety and protect the ecosystem, machines are not allowed to leave the unplowed, but packed, roads.

I put fresh wax on the skis and move back from the road until I am in a tree-walled corridor of shade and piney smells. The place looks familiar. Was it here that I saw a grizzly bear some summers back? Probably not. But grizzlies are in my thoughts, and have been ever since last night when a ranger told me that they are not true hibernators. They sleep most of the winter, granted, but it is not unusual for one to rouse himself and venture out in search of a meal. It depends on the weather. If the air temperature gets too warm — above, say, 45 degrees — the animal is up and stirring.

I would, of course, treasure the sight of a grizzly lumbering through this powder snow. But it's not to be, not today. I'll forget that and go with friends to the rim of the Grand Canyon of the Yellowstone. Skis are put aside. This is a trip for snowcoach.

More with tenacity than grace, the tracked vehicle moves through the mountain heights of the park in jarring lunges at erratic speed. That's all right, for there's a lot to see and it wouldn't do to hurry. When only a few miles along, we come upon Steven Fuller, a winter caretaker for the park company. He has been camping out for several nights and is now on his way back to the canyon where he lives with his wife and two young daughters. His mustache is crusted with ice, and his eyes are teary under the sting of cold.

However, he is like a man reborn, and no wonder. Overnight outings here, in winter, do that to a person. There are nights in this Rocky Mountain country when the sky is crystal with the flash of stars, when the air is so crisp and pure that a breath hangs on it like a smudge. There is no wind. Nothing stirs. On such nights is peace visited on those who sleep in the open.

The snowcoach is stopped. We must walk now to the point that gives the best view of canyon and river. It's uphill, and we work to gain footholds in the snow and ice. Blessedly, the weather has cleared again.

In summer, the walls of the canyon are reddish-yellow (thus their name). Now they are banked with snow, and the vast rent in the mountains is almost hypnotic in its whiteness. For about 20 miles it stretches at heights of more than 1,000 feet. Below, the Yellowstone is whipping back and forth along its eddying course, now and then undercutting the bank to fracture the snow and set off slides.

At one point, the river emerges from a lip of the canyon to drop 109 feet. This is the Upper Falls of the Yellowstone, surely one of the most dazzling leaps of water in the West. Emerging with such force that it arches through the air, the river hurls its spray against the rocks on either side and there it freezes to build on the curtains of pale blue ice.

There is a ritual among workers in the park who frequently come to this canyon viewing area. It is this: When descending the hill, one must get on one's back and slide down, head first. So I do it. I come racing down the hill backward and upside down, and as I do I look up to see a chalky skim move across the sun.

It's going to snow tonight.

On a winter evening, a bull elk grazes along a patch of snow-free grass by the Firehole River. Warmed by geyser runoff and hot springs, the plant-edged riverbanks attract hungry elk and bison in winter.

Geysers and hot springs create unstable landscapes. In eruption, Crater Hills Geyser (below) spills hot silica-laden waters over its rim. The silica cools and hardens to a crust resembling coral, or coats pebbles to form "geyser eggs." At Mammoth Hot Springs, lime-charged water seeps from a mountainside. As it cools, it deposits a fresh white glaze of lime that builds fast-growing terraces. From crest to foreground pools, the features opposite measure roughly 20 feet—the work of Minerva Spring, now the most active and currently considered the loveliest.

Year-round warmth of geyser basins supports a
microcosm of plant and animal life. Bright
yellow and green-spotted algae (right) flourish
in the hotter waters—food for myriads of tiny flies
that fall prey to the water spider. Mosses and
a miniature red mushroom thrive on heated soil;
a "pussytoes" plant a few inches tall reaches
cold air that veils it in frost. Hot runoff finding
new channels often kills lodgepole pines, but
wolf lichen grows on the dead wood.

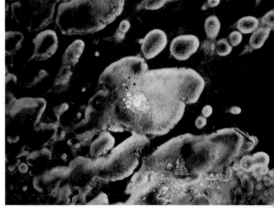

Alone on winter range in the Hayden Valley, where Elk Antler Creek runs clear, an

STEVEN FULLER

old bull bison nuzzles through two feet of snow to reach the shriveled grass beneath.

ℱood quest in winter: Canada geese fly above the Yellowstone River, ice-free near the falls. Bighorn rams, down from the Washburn Range, nibble juniper bark in the Lamar Valley; and a bull moose grazes beside the Gallatin River.

*O*verleaf: Park winter keepers Jean
and Jeremy Schmidt, with their visitor
Jill Durrance, ski through Upper
Geyser Basin in early morning. Steam
from Plume Geyser clouds the sun
as the boiling runoff flows beside the
trail. Old Faithful erupts at right.

"*We'd always wanted to do something like this,*" *say Dr. and Mrs. James R. Little of Jackson, Wyoming. They camped for three days near Norris Geyser Basin, ski-touring and snowmobiling through the thermal area and back country. Setting up camp, Jim pulls the nylon tent into place; Martha uses ski poles to fill a bucket at Solfatara Creek without slipping off the bank. At nightfall, they add water to a panful of freeze-dried turkey beside a glowing fire.*

*W*inter's icy touch transforms the natural features of Yellowstone—both large and small—with a white and crystalline splendor. Fairy Falls, near Midway Geyser Basin, cascades almost 200 feet through a thickening shield of frozen spray. The brilliant encasement of blue-white ice forms gradually as the water splashes outward in the freezing air. Jewel-like icicles hang from cone and twig on a lodgepole pine. Steam from nearby geysers condenses and freezes on branches and trunk until a shroud of hoarfrost disguises a new "ghost tree." Wrapped in the white fastness of winter, Yellowstone becomes a world of primeval beauty. Here wildlife wanders unhindered through a land of steaming geysers and snow-laden trees, surrounded by the age-old grandeur of the towering Rockies.

EPILOGUE

Of Wealth and Wilderness: The Values of the Future

*. . . the richest values of wilderness lie not
in the days of Daniel Boone, nor even in
the present, but rather in the future.*
ALDO LEOPOLD (1887-1948)

NOWHERE ELSE IN THIS NATION is concern for the future more intense
than it is in the Rocky Mountain West. And for good reason: Forces
for drastic change are banging away at the six-state region. Canada
as yet faces less urgent choices, enjoys more leisure to plan the future
of a region still relatively unspoiled.

Previews of where the Mountain West may be heading have
flashed in recent times, and, to many, the signs foreshadow the loss
of a way of life. Denver's air is foul, and emphysema sufferers are
fleeing the city, whereas 50 years ago the good air of that mile-high
place was a lure for the ailing. The town of Aspen is studying pro-
posals for a rapid-transit system—an electric, high-speed railway to
ease the congestion in a former mining camp. The mayor of Telluride
has had to hire an assistant to handle administrative duties in a town
that might be snowed in anytime during eight months of the year.

Ranches have been sold for resort developments. Snowmobiles
have shattered the splendid silence of the Yellowstone winter. Mon-
ster machines have ripped the earth to get at the coal. The waters of
the rivers have been overcommitted, and the public lands overgrazed.

Yet the Mountain West, as of now, remains submissive to its
wilderness. There is smog in the large cities, yes, and there is pollution in some of the streams, but the smell of pine is still stronger
than that of exhaust fumes, and for every gallon of stagnant, lifeless
water, there is a flood of snow melt tumbling over the slopes.

However, that doesn't speak for twenty years from now, or even

*Ignited oil shale flames in the Piceance Creek Basin, Colorado, site of the
world's largest known deposit. Such resources now create dilemmas for
region and nation: Development, or conservation? Profit, or quality of life?*

ten. Environmental flaws have a way of spreading, of feeding on themselves until the natural order of things tumbles out of gear. The bird songs stop, and the fish, poisoned by the acid in abused waters, surface in bloated death. Trees are stunted, wildflowers drained of color, and the skies are like butterscotch with industrial smoke.

It could happen. There are heavy designs on the sources of energy in the mountains. Coal is being strip-mined and used to make electricity. The companies involved in these operations are making efforts to put the land back in order, but the success of that has yet to be determined. It will be before the end of the century. Indeed, by the year 2000, the outcome will be clear on most of the issues now confronting the Mountain West. What will be done to stem the rising crime rate in Denver? Will cattle ranching survive as a business for any other than corporations? What changes in the social structures will be brought about as a result of protest movements by Indians and Chicanos and other minority groups?

Most of all, what damage, if any, will be inflicted on the quality of life? In, say, Durango, Colorado? There is a man in that town who runs a service station. I met him on a morning when I was setting out for Silverton, and as he ran a rag over the windshield of my car, he talked about his recently ended stay in southern California.

"I made a good deal of money there, working in an aircraft plant," he told me. "I gave it up to come here and work 12 hours a day for about half of what I was making. But the clean air is a bonus; the mountains are a bonus; the hunting and fishing are a bonus. Add all that up and I figure I'm ahead. The easy money I make here at the station feeds my stomach, and all those bonuses feed my soul."

Just a few miles from his station is a sprawling resort complex that cost many millions of dollars to build. There are others like it going up in other parts of the region. There will be more.

Resorts and recreation lure people. For commercial traffic, Denver's Stapleton International Airport is now among the ten busiest in the nation. They're coming not only to ski, but also to work. Some major companies have escaped the suffocating atmosphere of the eastern industrial areas by moving to the Rockies.

So, surely, growth is upon the Mountain West. It is upon Denver to such an extent that the city's lovely views of the Front Range are screened behind all the new construction when they're not disappearing in the smog. And the urbanization does not end with the Denver boundaries; it stretches north, for 65 miles, to Fort Collins, and more than 100 miles south, to Pueblo.

But leave that ribbon of growth and go west, go over the Continental Divide and down into the valleys; you'll find towns struggling for survival. In one, the school is down to one teacher and two students because the lumber company went out of business and almost everyone left. In another, there is no money to pay a policeman, and the single, aging patrol car sits rusting on the street.

There's that, and then there's Rock Springs, the town in Wyoming's coal-rich Sweetwater County being showered with prosperity.

There's Aspen with its hotels booked to capacity, and the nearby town of Lenado with its empty cabins and a main street being reclaimed by the trees. There's the vacationing family from the East in their $30,000 mobile home, and the Blackfeet Indian in his '57 pickup with the leaking radiator.

In the past, the states of the Rocky Mountains had but a weak voice in decisions involving their future. Outside influences — mining interests, the federal government, and others — were in control. That has now changed to a large degree.

"We decided nearly 200 years ago that the federal government would be supreme," says Richard Lamm, the governor of Colorado. "The constitutional law is clear. We can neither legally or morally keep people out. But we can stop selling Colorado and become selective with the type of jobs we want, and we can assert our interests vis-à-vis the federal government."

It is not likely that the states will ban strip mining of coal, but the companies are under strict controls as to methods of operation. That will continue. If anything, the controls will be tightened. For one thing, environmental groups are keeping close watch, and they are not hesitant about filing actions in court.

"It's unrealistic to think that we can keep all these sources of energy locked up," a rancher in Montana told me. "They're going to take the coal. In the old days there wouldn't even have been room for doubting that — they would have come in, taken what they wanted in the way they wanted, and the rest of us be damned. Not anymore. For the first time out here, I think, the outside companies have to accept local control. That's the key word in our future — control."

In most cases, the effectiveness of this control has been closely linked to unity of action among the six states. Therefore cohesiveness will probably strengthen, with more regional bodies, such as the Rocky Mountain Federation of Governors, taking form. Even with all their Congressmen voting together in the House of Representatives, the states have less political might than Los Angeles County.

Whatever happens between now and the end of the century, the Mountain West is not likely to lose its distinction as the heartland of wilderness in this country. And as I write these last words there is sadness upon me, for winter is settling in and I am not in the mountains. I am in Washington, and as I look out of my window it becomes painfully clear that Connecticut Avenue is not Wolf Creek Pass.

Wolf Creek Pass — ah, there must be three feet of fresh snow there already.

INDEX

Boldface indicates illustrations

Acknowledgments

"Laughing Bowl," by Donna Whitewing. From *The Whispering Wind*, edited by Terry Allen. Copyright © 1972 by The Institute of American Indian Arts. Reprinted by permission of Doubleday & Company, Inc.

Floral drawings for illuminated letters and for colophons by Josephine B. Bolt. Identifications: A—common gooseberry, B—Juneberry, D—mountain ash, F—wild plum, H—arrowheads, I—mountain sorrel, L—alpine avens, M—twinflower, N—sand lily, O—brook saxifrage, S—vetch, T—grass-of-Parnassus, U—Townsendia, V—marsh marigold, W—ricegrass; colophons: page 20—chokecherry, page 44—pericome, page 72—aspen, page 92—alpine spring beauty, page 116—common lupine, page 136—wild hops, page 156—fringed gentian, page 176—boulder raspberry, page 195—evening primrose. All are plants of the Rocky Mountains.

The Special Publications Division is grateful to the individuals, organizations, and agencies named or quoted in the text and to those cited here for their generous cooperation and assistance during the preparation of this book: the Denver Public Library; the Montana State Historical Society; the Smithsonian Institution; and R. L. Blackwell, Peter Decker, Ron Francis, Charles B. Hunt, Harry Perry, Paul A. Putnam, and William A. Weber.

Additional Reading

The reader may want to check the *National Geographic Index* for related articles, to refer to the Special Publications *The American Cowboy, American Mountain People, As We Live and Breathe: The Challenge of Our Environment,* and *Vanishing Wildlife of North America,* to the Society's book *Wilderness U.S.A.,* and to the following other books:

Wallace Atwood, *The Rocky Mountains;* Robert G. Athearn, *High Country Empire;* Ray Allen Billington, *The Far Western Frontier;* Isabella L. Bird, *A Lady's Life in the Rocky Mountains;* Hiram Chittenden, *A History of the American Fur Trade of the Far West;* John J. Craighead, Frank C. Craighead, Jr., and Ray J. Davis, *A Field Guide to Rocky Mountain Wildflowers;* Bernard DeVoto, *The Course of Empire;* John C. Ewers, *The Blackfeet Raiders of the Northwestern Plains;* S. David Freeman, *Energy: The New Era;* Carl B. Glasscock, *The War of the Copper Kings;* Aubrey Haines, *Yellowstone National Park;* Stuart S. Holland, *Landforms of British Columbia;* Charles B. Hunt, *Natural Regions of the United States and Canada;* Philip B. King, *The Evolution of North America;* David Lavender, *The Rockies;* Carey McWilliams, *North from Mexico;* David Muench, *Rendezvous Country;* Rocky Mountain Association of Geologists, *Geologic Atlas of the Rocky Mountain Region;* Marshall Sprague, *The Great Gates;* Wallace Stegner, *The Gathering of Zion;* Edward Norris Wentworth, *America's Sheep Trails.*

Library of Congress Ⓒ︎Ⓟ︎ Data
Ellis, William S   1927-
   The majestic Rocky Mountains.

   Bibliography: p. 197.
   Includes index.
   Ⓐ︎ Rocky Mountains region—Description and travel.   2. Ellis, William S., 1927-   Ⓘ Durrance, Dick. Ⓘ︎Ⓘ︎ National Geographic Society, Washington, D. C. Special Publications Division. Ⓘ︎Ⓘ︎Ⓘ︎ Title.
F721.E34   978   74-28807
ISBN 0-87044-178-7

Composition for *The Majestic Rocky Mountains* by National Geographic's Photo-typographic Division, Carl M. Shrader, Chief; Lawrence F. Ludwig, Assistant Chief. Printed and bound by Fawcett Printing Corp., Rockville, Md. Color separations by Colorgraphics, Inc., Beltsville, Md.; Progressive Color Corp., Rockville, Md.; J. Wm. Reed Co., Alexandria, Va.

46106

ELLIS

THE MAJESTIC ROCKY MOUNTAINS